BRITAIN IN OLD PHOTOGRAPHS

BRISTOL
1850–1919

DAVID J. EVELEIGH

SUTTON PUBLISHING LIMITED

Sutton Publishing Limited
Phoenix Mill · Thrupp · Stroud
Gloucestershire · GL5 2BU

First published 1996

Reprinted in 2002

Copyright © David J. Eveleigh, 1996

Cover photographs: *front*: interior view of the
study or drawing room in Blue Maids'
Orphanage, Ashley Hill, 1890s; *back*: William
Bailey, haulier on Feeder Road, St Philip's
Marsh, *c.* 1904–9.

British Library Cataloguing in Publication Data
A catalogue record for this book is available from the
British Library.

ISBN 0-7509-1300-2

Typeset in 10/12 Perpetua.
Typesetting and origination by
Sutton Publishing Limited.
Printed in Great Britain by
J.H. Haynes & Co. Ltd, Sparkford.

CONTENTS

Ships' masts, warehouses and ancient churches – the centre of Bristol with the tower of St Stephen's church an enduring landmark in an ever changing city; here the church is seen in May 1858, prior to restoration in 1860–61. The stone warehouses on Broad Quay were occupied by Dunlop, Mackie & Co., wine, spirit and porter merchants until about 1880. (J.W.G. Gutch)

INTRODUCTION

In 1908 the *Western Daily Press* ran a series of articles in the company's *Evening News* charting the progress made in the city since the 1850s. The following year the articles appeared as a single volume entitled *Bristol As It Was – And As It Is* and it was clear to its author, George Frederick Stone, that the progress achieved in that fifty-year span was unprecedented and quite unlike the slow, organic development that had previously characterised the city. Bristol had, in short, experienced a comprenhensive and dramatic transformation: the making of the modern city.

The photographs featured here coincide with this crucial phase in the creation of modern Bristol from the 1850s to the time of the First World War. In 1850 Bristol preserved the appearance of a late Georgian city with abundant remains from earlier phases in its history. Fragments of the city walls and castle survived as reminders of the city's medieval origins along with the towers of the old parish churches which rose above narrow streets of picturesque, gabled houses of the seventeenth century. The port and city were inextricably mixed: ships' masts were to be seen amongst the city streets – a sight that never failed to impress visitors – and much of the city's commercial life depended on coastal and overseas trade. The Bristol of 1850 was also dirty, insanitary and desperately short of clean drinking water. In 1845 sanitary inspectors had found in Bristol some of the worst living conditions in England and the third highest death rate.

In the decades that followed, the Victorians were to transform the physical environment of the city. The churches, mostly, survived – they were, of course, an essential part of the Victorian city – but much else was swept away with little sentiment and scant regard for conservation in a process of modernisation which established much of Bristol's present-day appearance and character. Narrow city thoroughfares were widened and timber-framed houses replaced with new factories, offices and shops. Fortunately, some old buildings lost as early as the 1850s, such as the Fourteen Stars Tavern, Counterslip, were recorded by camera before demolition. Streets were cleaned, sewers laid and lighting improved, first with gas and then electricity. An efficient urban transport system was established, local newspapers proliferated for an increasingly literate population and telephones made their debut – in 1879. In addition, a wide range of public services and amenities was introduced: from schools and hospitals to libraries, public baths and parks.

None of this, of course, was unique to Bristol: cities and towns throughout Britain were undergoing a similar process of modernisation. In Bristol, as elsewhere, it was a process often muddled and fumbling, achieved through an uneasy alliance of private enterprise and municipal intervention. Bristol was notable in that several major utilities, such as the supply of gas, water and the tramways, were in the hands of commercial concerns; nevertheless, this period marks the growing role of civic administration in determining the affairs of the city. From 1848 the docks were placed under municipal control and the generation of electricity (apart from the tramway's supply) was in the hands of the City Corporation. From the 1850s new committees charged with responsibility for public health and sanitation, education, cemeteries, open spaces and so forth were created, sometimes taking over functions previously vested in the old parish authorities, or often managing new areas – such as library provision – the result of national legislation.

Civic administration was thus extended citywide as the city itself rapidly widened its boundaries. Mid-nineteenth century maps show that the city's layout still related closely to the medieval plan. But after 1850, like other Victorian cities, Bristol rapidly expanded, aided by trains and trams, engulfing nearby farms and neighbouring villages. The suburbs were differentiated socially: the industrial areas of housing built to the east and south of the city acquired a very different character to the fashionable suburbs of Clifton, Cotham and Redland in the west and north. The expansion was accompanied by boundary changes in 1894, 1897 and 1904, adding more than 12,000 acres to its municipal area whilst the population grew by 222,000. These figures hide the experiences of thousands of individual Bristolians who lived through and contributed to this period of change, and whilst the part played by leading citizens – Sir George White, Joseph Storrs Fry and others – is well documented their achievements can overshadow the lives of many ordinary citizens.

This book, however, draws attention to some lesser-known Bristolians: James Cox, for example, blinded in a foundry explosion and as a result convinced of his duty to preach the word of God; William Bailey, a haulier from St Philip's Marsh who played his small part in distributing the remains of the city's horse population – once they had been boiled, ground and crushed – as manure and glue; a social contrast is provided by Dorothy and Frances Brewer, daughters of an accountant in the affluent suburb of Cotham, seen with their toy horse and dolls in about 1910. The prim figure on the left of the 1890s photograph in Blue Maids Orphanage on page 111 is almost certainly Isolene Lee, the matron of the orphanage, and the woman with her (featured on the front cover) is probably the schoolmistress, Ann Miller.

The survival of old photographs is largely a matter of chance and to some extent the availability of surviving photographs has determined the shape of this book. Some of the views are published here for the first time, but in order to achieve a balanced representation it has proved impossible to exclude some well-known views. Where the name of the photographer is known this is added at the end of the caption in brackets, and each picture is placed in the context of the main theme of this book – the making of the modern city of Bristol.

THE INNER CITY

The idea of an inner city was a consequence of nineteenth-century urban expansion. As Bristol acquired new suburbs, each with its own identity and character, the old city came to be known as the 'central district' or the 'ancient city'. The city had originated in Saxon times around a bridge over the Avon; the Saxon name was 'Brigstow' – the place of a bridge. The medieval city had developed between the Avon and Frome: a huddle of narrow streets in a cluster of parishes, some tiny, like All Saints', and each marked by a church tower creating one of the distinctive architectural features of the inner city.

The medieval town centred on the intersection of four main streets: the High Street and Broad Street, Corn Street and Wine Street. A High Cross stood at this junction until removed in 1733, although by the nineteenth century it no longer served as the centre. Indeed, it is a peculiarity of Bristol that it does not have a single, undisputed central focus. The new Victorian towns and cities of the midlands and north were designed around a physical centre, usually a square dominated by a town hall which clearly marked the town or city centre and asserted the supremacy of civic authority. Bristol's Council House – until the completion of the present building on College Green – was tucked away in Corn Street close to other prominent commercial buildings such as the Corn Exchange. Rather, Bristol had several focal points: Corn Street as the chief commercial street was one, the quayside in St Augustine's Reach another and in the late 1890s, when part of this was covered over, Bristol acquired the Tramway Centre: a raised triangle of pavement where the trams stopped. For a few decades this was Bristol's centre; but it was not a monument to civic authority – rather the centre of operations for the independently owned tramway company run by Sir George White – a frequent protagonist of the City Corporation!

Nevertheless, it was not privately run trams but the publicly owned City Dock that gave the centre its atmosphere and character. The non-tidal Floating Harbour – 83 acres in extent – which enabled ships to float at all times, rather than sink in the mud at low tide, had been completed by the independent dock company in 1809. Unfortunately, high port dues were charged to recoup the investment, making this one of the most expensive ports in the country. As ship owners turned to other ports with more competitive dues, public agitation found a powerful voice in the Free Port Association which, in 1848, succeeded in transferring the operation of the port to the Bristol Corporation. Immediately, the city introduced more moderate dues but the port continued to decline owing to the introduction of ever larger iron ships which could neither navigate the tortuous course of the Avon nor enter the Floating Harbour. In 1873 the entrance locks at the Cumberland Basin were enlarged but it was clear that, if Bristol was to continue to function as a major port, new deep water docks were essential. 'Dockisation' of the entire length of the Avon down river from Bristol was seriously contemplated but the ultimate solution was the creation of new docks initially run by private companies at the mouth of the Avon. In 1877 new deep water docks were opened at Avonmouth, followed two years later by a dock at Portishead.

In 1884 control of the new docks at the mouth of the Avon passed to the Docks Committee. It was here that the bulk of Bristol's ocean-going trade came to be concentrated. The decline of the City Docks, however, was a gradual process and throughout the rest of the nineteenth century tall-masted sailing ships could be found berthed in the heart of the city. To the usual scenes of street life could be added the fascinating spectacle of the forest of ships' masts, rigging and all the paraphernalia – warehouses, cranes and cargoes – of docking, rubbing shoulders with fashionable shops and ancient churches. The course of the Frome, realigned in the thirteenth century to provide improved berthing, brought ships as far as Stone Bridge, near St Mary-on-the-Quay. Here, in St Augustine's Reach, ships trading with Africa, the West Indies and America were crowded, unloading cargoes of raw materials: corn, tobacco, sugar cane and luxury goods such as tea and coffee which supplied the city's trades and industries. A few streets away, along the old course of the Avon as far as Bristol Bridge, tall-masted vessels could be found berthed at Welsh Back and Redcliffe Back, two old-established quays traditionally associated with the coastal trade of the Bristol Channel and South Wales. The names 'Welsh Back' and the 'Llandoger Trow' are reminders of this once important trade; the term 'Back' is believed to refer to the backs of merchants' houses which formerly lined the quayside. By the mid-nineteenth century the merchants had long since departed for more salubrious surroundings and the backs were chiefly lined with granaries, flour mills and other industrial premises.

Although the City Docks were in decline, developments still took place in the second half of the nineteenth century. A new corporation granary was built by the Docks Committee in 1887 overlooking St Augustine's Reach. New deep water berths were constructed at Princes Wharf and Whapping Wharf and given railway connections; further new stone quays were constructed at Dean's Marsh and around to Canon's Marsh. Smaller steamships also became a regular feature of the City Docks after 1850, and operating fast, regular schedules around the British Isles created a need for transit sheds where cargoes could be swiftly prepared and dispatched. Dublin Shed was built on Narrow Quay and 'E' Shed, designed by Edward Gabriel in 1894, was given an ornate elevation and iron gates facing St Augustine's Parade.

Whilst the docks contributed to the changing face of the inner city during the late nineteenth century, there were other more decisive factors at work. Foremost was the increasing volume of road traffic. Victorian and Edwardian photographs of Bristol show streets filled with a chaotic variety of traffic: hand carts, barrows and small horse-drawn delivery vans; then the larger horse-drawn carts, wagons and drays, and passenger vehicles including private carriages and vehicles for hire – two-wheeled hansom cabs and the more sedate four-wheeled growlers. As the city's population grew, traffic across the central area increased: from the 1870s tramlines added to the congestion along some routes and by the end of the century there were also hundreds of 'safety' bicycles on the roads. The old city streets, in many instances, were simply not wide enough to accommodate the extra traffic and their layout did not reflect the predominant flow. Nowhere was this more apparent than along the route from Clifton to the railway terminus at Temple Meads. The railway station opened in 1840 – rather out on a limb – east of the centre, and created extra traffic which was hampered by several restrictions. Attempts to improve the route to Temple Meads began soon after the station opened. As early as 1845 the Corporation proposed to construct a new thoroughfare to be called Victoria Street and to widen Bristol Bridge. Municipal resolve faltered at the cost and it was not until 1859 that work began on widening the east side of Bristol Bridge; Victoria Street followed in 1871, cutting through old property in Temple and Redcliffe; and then in 1873–4 the western side of the bridge was widened. The following year the Corporation decided to extend Baldwin Street, creating a straighter route between the Drawbridge and Bristol Bridge and alleviating pressure on Corn Street and Clare Street. The scheme went ahead in spite of opposition from 'influential citizens', who owned property in the way of the new road, and was opened with full civic pomp and ceremony on 1 March 1881. 'There are few Bristol thoroughfares', wrote Stone in 1909, 'on which fifty years have produced greater changes than Baldwin Street – practically the whole of its frontages are creations of the past 30 years.'

The worst restriction on this route was the inadequate crossing of St Augustine's

Reach by the Drawbridge at the bottom of Clare Street. The term drawbridge was something of a misnomer, as this was actually a swing bridge that was opened whenever a vessel needed to pass. The Corporation eventually reacted to years of mounting public frustration with the delays and queues it caused, and in 1892 the upper section of St Augustine's Reach beyond the drawbridge was covered over and the narrow drawbridge was replaced by a wide fixed bridge – St Augustine's Bridge – which effectively marked the new entrance to the culverted river Frome. The usefulness of the dock beyond the drawbridge had lessened owing to the increasing size of ships but its removal was opposed by the Docks Committee and individuals like Ernest Lorymer, a corn merchant, who successfully sued for the loss of access by water to his premises. Nevertheless, the issue was an indication of the diminishing influence of the docks on city affairs and also of the strength of voice of road users several years in advance of the arrival of motor vehicle traffic.

In the half century after 1850 the Street Improvement Committee made many other modifications to city streets. Redcliff Street, which was described as 'a disgrace to the city', was widened in 1874. Other road improvements resulted in the loss of much old property: the aptly named Steep Street, for example, narrow and picturesque, with its run-down seventeenth-century houses, had once formed part of the main route north-west out of the city but was demolished in 1871. Fortunately, its picturesque appearance attracted the attention of artists and also of photographers such as John Hill Morgan, whose superb views are reproduced here. The Dutch House, an imposing timber-framed house on the corner of Wine Street and the High Street, only just survived demolition in 1908 on the casting vote of the Lord Mayor, although the ground floor was still cut back to widen the road. The new buildings, offices and factories, that took their place helped to change the face of the city; they brought a new style of architecture –robust façades of round arches and arcades in polychrome brick, loosely Italianate in inspiration and somewhat inappropriately termed 'Bristol Byzantine'. The building of several new factories also resulted in large scale clearance in the central area: Fry's, for example, were responsible for the demolition of much old property around the Pithay. Fortunately, Fry's made a photographic record before demolition of the old buildings. After 1850 some of the worst slums in the city were also cleared by the Sanitary Committee, and for all these reasons the population of the central area fell. By the 1880s the population of Bedminster was greater than than that of the inner city.

Victorian Bristol was widely considered to be one of the worst lit cities in England. In 1893 'Lesser Columbus' (Leonard Cohen) described Bristol as the 'worst lighted city' in the United Kingdom. Gas lamps had made their debut on Bristol streets in 1817, but in 1850 some parts of the city remained without lighting altogether. Those streets with lamps were still gloomy for the standards were generally set too far apart and the simple flat flame burners of the lamps emitted a poor light. In 1891 the

Corporation's Electrical Committee recommended lighting the central streets with electric arc lamps. On 20 November 1893 the first lamps were brought into use on Bristol Bridge and in nearby streets. With 1,000 candle-power lights supported on elegant, tall standards, they were an immediate success; in 1898 the lamps were extended to Whiteladies Road and Clifton, and by the early 1900s they were a familiar item of street furniture throughout the city and the suburbs.

Mid-nineteenth century Bristol was also one of the dirtiest and most unhealthy cities in England. A Parliamentary Report on the Sanitary Condition of Bristol carried out in 1845 had found appalling squalor, especially in some of the crowded courts and alleys occupied by the poor in the centre of the city. Overcrowding, low standards of cleanliness, contaminated water from old wells and pumps and inadequate drainage were found in Lewin's Mead, Temple and St Philips. Raw sewage emptied into the stagnant waters of the Floating Harbour and into the Frome, which was particularly filthy between St John's Bridge and Quay Head. Here, the ramshackle privies of old houses overhung the river and deposited sewage directly on to the river mud. The stench was intolerable, especially in warm weather, and the insanitary conditions contributed to several serious outbreaks of cholera and typhoid between the 1840s and 1860s. In 1849 a cholera epidemic in Bristol caused 444 deaths.

Following the 1848 Public Health Act, a Local Board of Health was established in 1851 to begin the process of cleaning the city. From 1855 main sewers were laid and home owners were obliged to make connections to them. The creation of a system of drains and sewers was a major Victorian achievement: an invisible but supremely important part of the city's modernisation – transforming living conditions and reducing the mortality rate substantially between 1850 and 1870. By 1874 there were 43 miles of sewers in place carrying the sewage to the tidal Avon below the Cumberland Basin. Foul cesspits and other nuisances were also removed, crowded and disease-ridden slums gradually demolished and refuse collecting and street cleaning improved. After 1847 homes began to receive piped water supplies from the Bristol Water Company and the old inadequate pumps and wells were removed. The results were dramatic: the death rate in Bristol fell from twenty-nine per thousand in 1845 to twenty by 1880, and in 1869 The Times described Bristol as one of the healthiest towns in Great Britain.

The Victorians reshaped Bristol in a slow and piecemeal process, but succeeded in preserving the dense cityscape that was only undone during and after the Second World War; nevertheless, much of Victorian Bristol remains with us now, testimony to the scale and permanence of their achievement.

Bristol Bridge from Welsh Back, 1850s. Bristol acquired its name in Saxon times from the bridge spanning the Avon here. The bridge marked the limit upstream accessible to sea-going ships and only barges and other small craft could continue eastwards to the expanding industrial suburbs of St Philip's Marsh and beyond. A medieval stone bridge of 1247 was replaced between 1764 and 1768 by this elegant three-arched and balustraded bridge designed by James Bridges; however, by the 1850s it was proving too narrow to cope with the expanding volume of road traffic between the centre and Temple Meads railway station. In 1861 the eastern side was widened by adding a cantilevered pavement supported on columns, resulting in the removal of the Portland stone balustrade and toll houses at each end. The remaining pair of toll houses were removed in 1873–4 when the west side of the bridge was widened. The boats in the foreground are tied up at Welsh Back and the factory chimneys in the background belong to Conrad Finzel's sugar refinery on Counterslip.

St Nicholas's church with Bristol Bridge in the foreground, between 1913 and 1920. The extra width to the bridge achieved by adding cantilevered pavements each side is clearly visible in this view as two Brislington-bound trams cross. The statue of Samuel Morley, a Liberal Member of Parliament for Bristol from 1868 to 1885, was erected beside St Nicholas's church in 1887 and moved to the Haymarket in 1921 to ease traffic congestion.

High Street, May 1858. The Druid Arms next to St Nicholas's church was demolished for the widening of Nicholas Street in 1864; the Angel Inn, next door, having lost its centuries-old neighbour, then collapsed! Seventeenth-century timber-framed gabled houses interspersed with Georgian buildings mainly of brick typified mid-nineteenth century Bristol streets: many were to go as the Victorians made their mark. (J.W.G. Gutch)

High Street, c. 1912. Insurance offices built in 1866 occupy the corner of Nicholas Street, while electric arc street lighting, overhead tram wires, a letter box, telephone sign and a monument to Liberalism (the Morley statue) all testify to Victorian progress.

The Dutch House, corner of Wine Street and High Street, c.1909. This was actually a Bristol merchant's house of about 1676. In 1908 a recommendation that it should be removed to widen the road was only defeated by the casting vote of the Lord Mayor. Instead, it was refurbished and the ground floor cut back to allow some road widening; the photograph was taken shortly after this was completed. The house remained a curiosity of Bristol until destroyed in the Blitz of 24 November 1940.

St Augustine's Reach, with a three-masted barque moored on the left alongside St Augustine's Parade,1868. Bristol Quay along the channel of the Frome brought ocean-going merchant ships into the heart of the city, creating the forest of ships' masts amongst the streets which so impressed visitors. Fred Little captured this sight at about the time the docks entered a slow decline; the Floating Harbour could only accept the smaller types of steam-powered vessel so new, deep water docks were opened downstream at Avonmouth in 1877 and Portishead in 1879.

Welsh Back, *c.* 1875. The churches of All Saints, Christ Church, St Nicholas and, further right, St Mary-le-Port, and a chimney-stack belonging to J.S.Fry's, form a backdrop to sailing vessels berthed at Welsh Back on the left and at Redcliff Back, right. There are no steamships in the scene although a 'lighter' (a barge requiring towing), possibly laden with grain, might be going further up river. The covered sheds, warehouses and the impressive brick granary of Wait & James, corn and flour merchants, designed by Ponton & Gough in 1869 and seen on the left, are evidence of the industrialised aspect of this section of the Floating Harbour.

Broad Quay and the Drawbridge from St Augustine's Parade, *c.* 1875. The Drawbridge just visible on the left, built in 1868, was actually a swing bridge and was often the cause of congestion on this important route between Clifton and Temple Meads. In 1864 a survey of traffic showed that from 5 a.m. in the morning to 10 p.m. 30,318 passengers, 1,634 carriages, 1,382 carts and 130 horses crossed the bridge.

St Augustine's Bridge and the Tramway Centre, *c.* 1910. Until 1892 sea-going vessels entering St Augustine's Reach were able to go as far as Stone Bridge near Small Street, and road traffic had to cross by the narrow Drawbridge. In May 1893 a wider, fixed crossing – St Augustine's Bridge – was opened to relieve traffic congestion and the Frome was covered over beyond the new fixed crossing; thus, several years before the appearance of motor vehicles on Bristol's streets, the demands of road traffic predominated over those of dock users.

Tramway Centre, between 1908 and 1910. Following the covering over of the Frome beyond St Augustine's Bridge, gardens were laid out in Colston Avenue and the Tramways Centre established. The trams stopped alongside a triangular paved area overlooked by the offices of the Bristol Tramways & Carriage Company in the gabled building with its well-known clock, which was added in about 1900. Horse-drawn trams first ran on Bristol streets in 1875 and were an immediate success; however, they were slow and struggled against the city's many gradients – even with the aid of additional trace horses. Electric trams were introduced in 1895: they made light of the hills and by 1900 the horses had gone. The electric trams were effective shifters of people and were important in bringing the expanding suburbs within reach of the centre. In 1908 each day, from 5.30 in the morning to 11.30 at night, 1,666 trams left the Tramway Centre for the suburbs with a passenger capacity in excess of 99,000.

The BTCC was also the major provider of cabs and in 1908 introduced motor taxis, although the last horse cab was not withdrawn until 1910. Here a four wheel horse-drawn 'growler' is seen at the taxi rank in the foreground. An electric advertisement for Bovril surmounts the roof of Insall & Sons, St Augustine's Parade, leading portmanteau and trunk makers in the city since 1829.

The Tramway Centre from 'E' Shed, late 1890s. An unusual view of the tramway centre through the imposing gateway to 'E' Shed, a dockside shed designed by Edward Gabriel in 1894, which the port authorities decided should hide its utilitarian character behind an embellished façade facing the Tramway Centre and College Green.

Old Market, 1897 or 1898. A busy scene in this important city thoroughfare soon after the Bristol Tramways & Carriage Company first introduced electric trams on the route from Old Market to Kingswood in 1895. Old Market was the second largest transfer point with four tracks and ample reversing and crossing facilities. The tram in the centre, resplendent in the Company's dark blue and ivory white livery is heading towards Kingswood pulling former horse-drawn car 103, whilst car 127 (left) heading for Eastville is one of a batch of low height trams specially built to pass under the railway bridge in Fishponds Road. Streets on the tramway company's routes, as seen here, were transformed by the addition of the web of wires carried aloft on elegant poles.

Two horse-drawn bakers' vans are stopped alongside T. Snow & Sons, grocers, next to the exotic Moorish style façade of the White Hart Hotel; this provided access and doubtless many a quick drink for those on their way to the Empire Theatre of Varieties, which opened in 1893. Next door again is the ironmonger's and cutler's shop of John Rich, established in 1839.

Redcliff Hill looking towards St Mary Redcliffe, *c*. 1910. Edwardian Redcliff Hill was a bustling thoroughfare with electric trams linking the city with Bedminster. Graceful tram poles, different to those in Old Market, support the tram wires. A wide variety of shops and businesses lined the street, including a saddler, tinsmith, oil and colour man, refreshment rooms and public houses, food, clothes and chemists' shops.

Clare Street, *c*. 1910. The business centre of the city where many banks, insurance offices and solicitors were located. On the right the Yorkshire Insurance Company occupies offices above Glass & Co., tobacconists, whilst opposite the Sun Fire Office displays two large trademarks based on firemarks, which used to be attached to insured properties. Silk hat making was an important city trade located in the fashionable parts of the centre, and further down the street is the sign of Daniel Parsley, hat maker.

Blue Bowl Inn, Pithay, between 1870 and 1876. John Williams, whose name appears on the signboard, was the last landlord of the Blue Bowl Inn from 1870 to 1876, and this photograph from the Fry's company archive probably dates from 1876, shortly before it was pulled down to make way for Fry's number three factory. The man standing in front of the doorway is Thomas Denford, who worked for Fry's as an engine fitter (from 1869) and building works manager; he is holding some rolled paperwork – perhaps the drawings of the new factory – and may have been in charge of the demolition of the inn.

The Fourteen Stars Tavern, Counterslip, pre-1857. Carriers were usually located beside inns and here we see Bennett's warehouse making the most of its association with the modern steam railway and apparently dwarfing the Fourteen Stars, a frail survivor from the seventeenth century. Bennett began business in 1836 as a road carrier operating spring vans to London; by 1842 he was agent to the Great Western Railway 'forwarding to all stations on their line'. The tavern was demolished in 1857 to make way for Finzel's sugar refinery. (H. Owen)

Chapel Court, Pithay, between 1898 and 1902. A Dickensian scene of working men and boys standing amongst barrels of American crystal glucose, probably for use by Fry's in chocolate confectionery, in this cramped court enclosed by seventeenth- and eighteenth-century buildings soon to be swept away for the construction of Fry's factory number eight. The court took its name from the Baptist chapel of 1791, which is just visible on the extreme left and was used by Fry's in the late nineteenth century as a factory to make wooden boxes.

Bottom of Pithay, *c*.1880. The houses on the right recall Celia Fiennes's description of Bristol in 1698: 'The buildings of the town are pretty high, most of timber work, the streets are narrow and something darkish because the roomes on the upper storys are more jutting out.' The houses on the right were demolished to make way for Fry's factory number four in about 1880. The ground floor windows are boarded up and many window panes have been smashed.

The Frome under Union Street, 12 September 1871. Until the mid-nineteenth century the course of this river through the city was little more than an open sewer; the privies of old houses lining the river emptied directly into it causing a dreadful stench and spreading diseases such as cholera and typhoid. In stages, between 1857 and 1867, the course of the Frome through the city centre was covered over creating two new thoroughfares – Rupert Street and Fairfax Street – whilst the Board of Health Committee formed in 1851 started a major clean-up of the city, laying sewers, cleaning the streets and clearing the worst of the city's slums.

This photograph from the Fry's archive shows the recently culverted river by the Union Street bridge, one of thirteen that once spanned the river in the city. The man on the left is W. Clarke, a Fry's employee, and the man on the right is Thomas Denford who also worked for Fry's (see page 22). Denford's 'Time Books' for the early 1870s survive, and record that from late August until the week ending 13 September 1871 he had two labourers, H. Cox and W. Lovell, paving a yard and culvert: this is probably the work being carried out here. It is less clear why the fashionable Bristol photographer G. Guttenburg should record this fairly mundane job! Denford lived at 32 Victoria Street near Stapleton Road from the early 1870s and died in 1903 aged about seventy-three. (G. Guttenburg)

Leonard Lane, off Corn Street, 1850s. The worst slums were found in the centre in old properties like these, dating from the seventeenth century or earlier; most had been cleared by 1900. (John Bevan Hazard)

Houses in Narrow Weir, between 1887 and 1894. The weir was a tributary of the Frome and once diverted water to a mill in Castle Mill Street. J. Llewellin, firework maker, occupied premises here from 1887 to 1894; the building he occupied was demolished in the early 1900s.

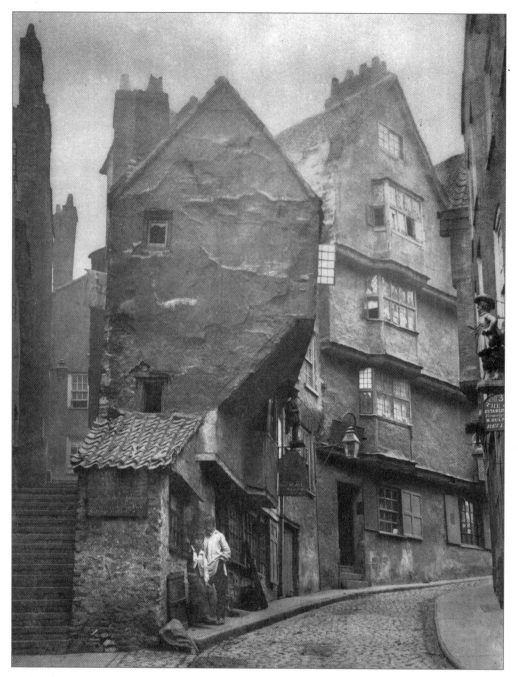

Steep Street, 1866. Until demolition by the City's Street Improvement Committee in 1871, travellers leaving the city for Gloucester and Wales via the Aust ferry had to climb the appropriately named Steep Street. In this view the signs of two chimney sweeps stare each other out across the street. (J.H. Morgan)

Steep Street from the junction with Trenchard Street (right) in 1866. These two views were photographed by John Hill Morgan of Parklands, Tyndalls Park, and published as a limited edition of 100 in 1891 by Frost & Read, 8 Clare Street and 47 Queens Road, Clifton. (J.H. Morgan)

All Saints Street, *c.* 1880. Backs of old houses soon to be demolished to make way for Fry's factory number four, completed in 1885. Joseph Storrs Fry (1826–1913) is seen fourth from left wearing a top hat and further right is Thomas Deuford who also appears in the views on pages 22 and 26.

The Prince of Wales public house, Tower Lane, Pithay end, 1896 or 1897. According to the sign Alfred E. Gazzard was the landlord here – one of the many public houses owned by Georges & Co., the largest brewers in Bristol by the late nineteenth century. Their beers, ales and stouts are advertised prominently, while a poster in the window advertises a show at the Tivoli Palace, a tavern music hall in Broadmead which opened in 1870 as the Alhambra and closed in 1900. (T. Protheroe, Wine Street, Bristol)

The Royal Hotel, College Green, 1870s. The photograph was taken on a warm summer's evening; the sun is in the west and a man reads by an open window to the left of the hotel entrance. It probably dates to within a few years of the building of the hotel in the mid-1860s as the stonework looks very clean. The prospectus of the College Green Hotel Company was launched in October 1863 with a capital of £40,000 in £10 shares and the hotel opened in March 1868. In April 1871 the national census enumerators found the hotel contained a resident staff of over thirty, including a French cook, kitchen maids, scullery maids, housemaids, porters and even a billiard marker, waiting on seventy-one guests, amongst whom were an MP, a colonel, several barristers, bankers, north country manufacturers and a ship owner.

College Green, an old-established open space, was altered considerably after 1850. In that year a replica high cross was located at the apex of the lawn. In the mid-1860s part of a Georgian row of houses overlooking the green was demolished to make way for the hotel; to the right of the hotel a signboard is faintly visible below the window of one of the surviving Georgian houses advertising G.E. Lomas, an importer of foreign wines and West Indian pickles, preserves and arrowroot from 1844 to 1879. In the 1880s a larger, ornate gas lamp replaced the one seen here, whilst the cross was moved to the centre of the green to make way for the Jubilee statue of Queen Victoria, erected in 1888. The churchyard of St Augustine's church, just visible on the left, was cut back in 1894 to improve access to College Green from the central area. The hotel's stonework, meanwhile, gradually darkened in the grimy city atmosphere.

A roof-top view of Redcliffe Street from St Mary Redcliffe looking towards the centre, *c.* 1879. Beyond the shops and Fairbrother's Temperance Hotel in the foreground, warehouses, granaries and mills dominate the skyline although the spire of St Nicholas is just visible through the gloom. Glass cones on Redcliff Back and the masts of ships in the Floating Harbour add to the variety of the scene.

The leaning tower of Temple church rises behind the Shakespeare inn of 1636 and other seventeenth- and eighteenth-century houses in Victoria Street in the 1870s. The gabled houses in the centre were subsequently demolished to make a through way to Church Lane.

Victoria Street, between 1874 and 1895. A horse and wagon loaded with barrels followed by a horse-drawn tram approach the camera in Victoria Street. Temple Meads, the main railway terminus, was situated well outside the old central area and only reached after a circuitous journey. In 1871 a new direct route was created by cutting a swathe through late medieval property between Bristol Bridge and the station. In the early 1870s the thoroughfare called – predictably enough – Victoria Street was filled with imposing shops and warehouses of polychrome brick in an Italianate style, generally known as 'Bristol Byzantine'. Sadly, many were lost during and after the Second World War and only a few remain, mostly in a very forlorn state. All those visible in this view, including W. Parnall & Co.'s shop fittings store on the right at 108 Victoria Street, have gone.

Neptune in Victoria Street, c. 1910. The statue of Neptune cast in lead by the Bristol founder Joseph Rendell was first erected in Temple Street in 1723 and moved on two further occasions, each time finding himself in the way of building or road alterations. His fourth move to the junction of Temple Street and Victoria Street took place in 1872; he remained here until relocated to his present resting place overlooking St Augustine's Reach in 1949.

Shops at Temple Gate, 1892. Nearest the camera is Amelia Mapstone's newsagent and confectioner
shop, covered in enamel signs and posters for local and national newspapers. Between this shop and the
Terminus Tavern in the background are a boot and shoe maker, a hair cutting saloon, Charles Crocome
refreshment rooms and a tobacconist.

Approach to Temple Meads railway station with BCTC Blue Taxi, registration AE 1847 leaving the
station, c. 1910. The joint railway station of the Great Western Railway and the Midland Railway was built
between 1865 and 1878, replacing the original Brunel terminus of 1840 seen on the left.

TRADE & INDUSTRY

Writing of Bristol in 1893, 'Lesser Columbus' called the city the 'Universal Provider'. 'There is scarcely anything', he wrote, 'that is not made in Bristol.' The variety and range of trades and industries in Bristol was considerable: mid-nineteenth century Bristol trade directories list over 300 trades and manufactures. Many important British industries were present in the city: coal mining, iron founding, heavy engineering, pottery and glass making, chemical industries, brewing, food processing, tanning and leather trades, cotton and a variety of clothing trades. As the financial centre of the region, Bristol was an important centre for banking and there were, besides, a whole multitude of retail trades supplying household goods and services. Within this range there were enormous contrasts: between large companies mass producing goods such as soap and candles, paper bags, chocolates and cigarettes using machinery and hundreds of semi-skilled workers in modern factories; and smaller businesses, often working in old, cramped workshops, relying on a relatively small, highly skilled and specialised workforce. Many of the city's trades and industries were interdependent: thus stoneware and glass bottle makers supplied containers to local brewers and manufacturers of soda water, ginger beer and lemonade; various engineering concerns were closely associated; and the relationship between Mardons who made cigarette packets for W.D. & H.O. Wills was so close that when the Imperial Tobacco Company was set up in 1901 to consolidate the interests of British manufacturers against the American Tobacco Company, Mardons joined the following year. No single industry dominated, however, and whilst some older industries declined others grew to take their place.

The port was vital to Bristol industry. Imports predominated: bulky raw materials such as corn, tobacco, sugar cane, timber, tallow and vegetable oils unloaded in the docks supplied the many factories situated around the docks. West India merchants imported luxury goods such as tea, coffee and spices which were sold by grocers in the city. In 1850 the tonnage of coastal shipping was greater than overseas; this was to change, however; parity was reached in 1890 and by 1914 foreign imports far outstripped coastal tonnage. The docks also generated business for the shipbuilding yards and for other ancillary trades such as sail makers, anchor smiths, ships' joiners and carvers. Bristol had an established reputation for excellence in shipbuilding and the building of the *Great Britain* in 1843 indicated that Bristol shipbuilders were capable of building modern ships of iron; nevertheless, after the 1850s the industry lost ground as the demand increased for ships larger than the Floating Harbour could accommodate. The late nineteenth century saw the closure of many yards, and by 1919 only Charles Hill & Son's Albion yard remained of any importance.

Other old-established Bristol industries slowly disappeared from the mid-nineteenth century. Sugar refining had been important in the city since the seventeenth century but declined in the nineteenth century as the industry switched to London, Liverpool and Glasgow, where unloading charges were lower. When Conrad Finzel's large refinery on the Counterslip failed in 1881 large scale refining in the city came to an end, and all refining ceased in 1908. Glass and brass making were two other industries important in the eighteenth and early nineteenth centuries that declined after 1850. Coal production from the collieries at Bedminster, Ashton and Easton reached a peak of 500,000 tons in 1875, but a rapid decline then followed and most of the mines had gone by the mid-1920s.

The city's economy, nevertheless, showed adaptability and resilience in the face of the decline of some of the older industries; new industries developed to take their place and in the second half of the nineteenth century Bristol underwent steady, if unspectacular, growth and in various ways the industries contributed to the process of modernisation. The period was notable for the expansion and consolidation of several major firms. In brewing, for example, the industry came to be dominated by Georges & Co., a business dating from the late eighteenth century that bought up other brewers and hundreds of public houses. (By the 1920s Georges had more than 700 tied houses in the Bristol region.) The old breweries once taken over were closed and Georges premises in Bath Street were successively enlarged. Christopher Thomas & Sons came to dominate the manufacture of soap and candles, and whilst several small firms continued in business none could match their output; in the 1870s this amounted to about 8 per cent of the national total. The larger companies expanded mass production, using large labour forces on a scale previously unknown in the city. Several thousand women and girls were employed in tobacco and chocolate industries – particularly in jobs requiring sorting and packing. In 1883 the *Bristol Times and Mirror* reported that the Great Western Cotton Works at Barton Hill employed 1,200 women and girls – 75 per cent of the total. The newspaper described how at certain times of the day the neighbourhood was filled with 'women and girls with headgear consisting of shawls, mostly of a red and white plaid . . . converging to or diverging from the portals of the cotton factory'.

Mass production was also achieved through the use of machinery. Established in 1786, Wills became the largest tobacco company in Bristol, producing pipe tobacco, cigars and cigarettes from 1871. The success of Wills's Wild Woodbines, introduced in 1888, was only made possible after the company acquired the British patent of the American Bonsack cigarette making machine, which could produce 1,500 cigarettes in eight minutes – as many as a hand operative would make in a day. Similarly, the expansion of the stationery and packaging industry was accelerated once machinery was in place. Elisha Smith Robinson started business in 1844 making paper bags by hand, but soon turned to machinery which vastly increased production; the success was such that in 1876 the company built new premises in Victoria Street to house more machines.

New factory buildings helped change the face of the city. They were not insignificant prefabricated buildings best hidden out of town on trading estates, but impressive structures intended to enhance the city. Robinson's new building in Victoria Street, designed by W.B. Gingell, was a stately building worthy of its location overlooking Bristol Bridge. Christopher Thomas & Bros, the Bristol Wagon Works and W.D. & H.O. Wills and other companies also built ornate factories, which, with their domes and cupolas, Italianate arches and polychrome brickwork created the distinctive 'Bristol Byzantine' style. The new factories were invariably steam powered, and by 1900 the large number of tall factory chimneys on the skyline gave parts of Bristol the appearance of a northern mill town.

New industries brought new skills. Besides innovations in printing and packaging by Mardons and Robinsons, light engineering – particularly in the field of transport – grew during the second half of the nineteenth century. Locomotive building in Bristol, notwithstanding a temporary collapse during the recession of the late 1870s, developed with two companies, the Avonside Engineering Company and Pecketts, establishing a reputation for cheap, robust shunting engines. With their distinctive copper-capped chimneys and brass domes, these were prettier than most. Railway carriages and wagons built by the Bristol Wagon Works enjoyed a worldwide reputation, and in 1900 Bristol entered the motor vehicle industry. Within a few years Sir George White, director of the tramway company, had attached the city's name to aeroplane design.

Some industries greatly added to the whole fabric of city life. The gas industry contributed to a better lit city and from the 1880s started supplying gas cookers on cheap weekly rents. The newspapers catered for an increasingly literate public and provided a forum for the discussion of contemporary issues – many of the developments featured in this book were the subject of robust correspondence in local newspapers. Their surveys of local industries, obituaries of leading citizens and historical features – like the 'Bristol As It Was – And As It Is' series carried in the *Evening News* in 1908–9 – all helped to strengthen the feeling amongst ordinary citizens of being part of Bristol.

Industry in Victorian and Edwardian Bristol was characterised by a strong local identity; of all the major employers only the Great Western Railway was based outside the city. The others were Bristol companies led by local families whose members exerted a strong personal influence on their workplaces and employees. Joseph Storrs Fry (1826–1913) arrived at the company's works in his brougham every morning at ten minutes to nine and then at nine o'clock read to his employees from the Bible. Other company directors were known personally by their workforces, and when they died the whole city mourned. Many individual company heads sat on committees of the City Council and were closely involved in the municipal improvements to the city, and several were elected mayor. Mark Whitwill, Sir George White, the Frys, the Wills and other leading industrialists were heavily involved in good works, personally financing new educational, health and recreational amenities in the city; several were also deeply committed to missionary work amongst the poor. The contribution of local industrialists towards the modernisation of the city was thus far greater than the development alone of trade and industry.

View from St Mary Redcliffe looking over the Floating Harbour to Bristol Bridge, believed to have been taken in 1872 from the scaffolding erected to complete the spire. The industrial character of Victorian Redcliffe is clearly seen with several factory chimneys rising above the roof tops between the harbour and Redcliffe Street on the right. Vessels of various kinds crowd the quayside at Welsh Back. The massive bulk of Proctor Baker's granary and mill with its large, square chimney-stack dwarfs the neighbouring industrial premises on Redcliff Back. Opposite, across the harbour on Welsh Back, is the equally imposing granary belonging to Waite & James, designed by the Bristol architects Ponton & Gough in 1869.

View from St Mary Redcliff looking towards Temple Church in 1872. The view emphasises the densely packed townscape of the parishes of Redcliff, Temple and St Thomas south of the Avon. In the nineteenth century the area contained several important industries including corn mills, pottery and glass kilns, Wills's tobacco works and Robinson's printing and stationary business.

These parishes also contained a large working population. Behind the principal streets there were many crowded courts and alleyways where some of the worst slum conditions in the city existed. They were the homes of labourers and dock porters and others such as millers and potters employed in the local industries: in 1871 Hamilton Court, for example, off St Thomas Street, was inhabited by several labourers, a shoe-maker, a railway man, a painter, haulier and woollen draper's assistant. There were also basket-makers, harness-makers, wheelwrights, pipe-makers and many other small tradespeople living in the area, reflecting the diversity of commercial and industrial activity in Victorian Bristol.

Pottery cones on Temple Back are visible in the distance. St Thomas Street runs diagonally from the top left until it joins Phippen Street in the right foreground. Buildings in Portwall Street occupy the rest of the foreground and conspicuous bottom left is the Methodist Free Chapel built in 1859; next to it are the premises of Lucy Rowe, a forty-two-year-old widow in 1871, who, with the help of one assistant and a general servant, made a living as a rag dealer and bottle merchant – the roof of her bottle store can be clearly seen.

Redcliff Wharf, *c.* 1878. Redcliff Back was one of the oldest wharfs in Bristol, dating from the middle ages. *Lookout*, a three-masted barque of 216 tons gross with a wooden hull, 112 ft long, was built in Workington in 1858; this was a typical mid-Victorian vessel, characteristic of the ocean-going vessels found trading in the old harbour in the city in the third quarter of the nineteenth century. From 1869 to 1878 she belonged to Lucas Brothers, African merchants, who in 1878 owned eight other barques and a brig – a two-masted square rigger.

Lucas Brothers traded with West Africa, the source of palm oil used to make soap, ivory and cocoa. The family business was started by William Lucas in Marsh Street in about 1823. By 1851 the business was based at Bathurst Basin where it remained until about 1877, when operations were moved to Redcliff Wharf. This photograph dates from either the spring of 1877, when the ship was in port between voyages to the West Coast of Africa, or the summer of 1878 upon her return. Shortly afterwards she was sold to W.H. Williams of Newquay, Cornwall, and continued in use until about 1896. Lucas Brothers ceased trading in about 1907. Members of the family were active citizens serving on the Council and as Merchant Venturers. John Lucas, one of the partners, lived at Redland Bank, which is illustrated on page 80.

Behind the wharf on Redcliff Hill is the shot tower built by William Watts, a Redcliff plumber in 1782. Lead shot was first made here by Watts's patent which involved molten lead falling the height of the tower into a vat of a cold water where the droplets solidified. At the time of this view the works were owned by Sheldon Bush & Co., patent shot and lead pipe manufacturers. This well-known Bristol landmark was demolished for road widening in 1968.

Souvenir postcard of the opening of the Royal Edward Dock, opened by King Edward VII and Queen Alexandra on 9 July 1909. This new dock was constructed as a response to the ever increasing size of cargo steamers and consisted of a huge basin reached by a lock 875 ft long, large enough to take any vessel in existence. The opening was the occasion for lavish public demonstration of civic pride, which is reflected here on this postcard.

Albion ship yard, c. 1910. The terraced housing of Southville forms a backdrop to the Albion ship yard, the most important and long lasting in Bristol, although here there is little apparent activity on either the launching way on the right or in the dry dock. The yard was founded by the Hillhouse family and owned by Charles Hill & Sons from 1848. The clock tower of the main office dominates the view and the manager's house, covered in creeper, is visible further to the left.

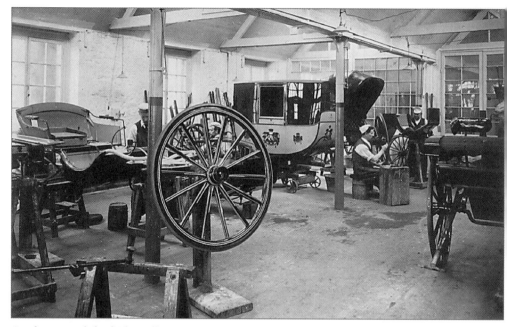

Coach painting loft of John Fuller & Co., St George's Road, *c.* 1910. Coach and carriage building was an important and old-established industry in Bristol. James Fuller took over Harper & Wolf's coach building business in 1815. The trade was highly skilled and specialised; the painting of carriages was a slow process with as many as eight or ten coats of paint and varnish applied, each one smoothed and polished before the next was added to achieve a durable and glossy finish.

Workforce of the Bristol Motor Company, Redcross Street, *c.* 1906. Bristol's first motor car was made in 1900 and the Bristol Motor Company was established by Arthur Johnson and William Appleton in 1902. The workshop equipment seen here powered by overhead line shafting includes a pillar drill, lathe and mechanical hacksaw.

Bill-head of Gardiner Sons & Co., ironfounders and ironmongers, 1916. Entering business in 1860, Gardiners soon became leading wholesale and retail ironmongers in the city, supplying a wide range of fireplaces, kitchen equipment, sanitaryware and other domestic hardware besides manufacturing architectural iron and brasswork. The company remains in business today as a DIY and furnishings store.

Llewellins & James brass foundry, Castle Green, 1889. There were several brass founders and coppersmiths in Bristol in the second half of the nineteenth century and Llewellins & James were by far the largest. In 1866 they employed about a hundred men and boys in the manufacture of bells, engineers' and plumbers' brassware, brewery equipment, gas light fittings and domestic copperware.

Fry's factories, between 1898 and 1902. New factories of J.S. Fry & Sons, chocolate manufacturers, in gleaming cream and red brick rise above old pantiled roofs in the Pithay. Fry's traced their foundation to 1728 and expanded dramatically after the 1850s to become one of the largest companies in Bristol. Number two factory, on the right, was built in 1860 and from then until 1914 a further ten factories were added to meet the expanding trade. Most of the works were situated in this cramped city centre location centred around the Pithay until 1923, when the company began the move to a new greenfield site at Somerdale, Keynsham. Number three factory is in the centre and number four, dated 1885, is on the left; factory bridges linked the individual blocks. Number three factory was demolished in 1937, number two the following year, but the left-hand chimney remained a city centre landmark until January 1961. (Lewis R. Protheroe, 3 Narrow Wine Street)

Girls counting and arranging chocolates in fancy boxes and bags at J.S. Fry & Sons, *c*.1908. As the popularity of eating-chocolate grew in the late nineteenth century, so the company's output rose and after 1885, Fry's produced more chocolates than cocoa. The number of Fry's employees rose from 193 in 1867 to 4,600 in 1908, including over 2,000 women and girls engaged mainly in wrapping and covering.

Cigar manufacture, W.D. & H.O. Wills, *c*.1912. Established in 1786, Wills became the largest tobacco company in Bristol producing pipe tobacco, cigars and, from 1871, cigarettes. Women are seen here working under electric arc lamps packing Rajah cigars; by 1901 Wills's workforce totalled 3,000. (Veal & Co.)

Laundry team,1890s. The exact location in this photograph is unknown, although it is believed to be a Bristol scene showing a group of laundry workers in a rather untidy backyard: the man on the left is holding a laundry stick, three women are holding newly starched collars, shirt fronts and bonnets whilst another three, wearing heavy aprons, are holding scrubbing brushes.

Telling Room, Capital & Counties Bank, c. 1895. This company opened its first Bristol branch in Victoria Street in 1878, moving to Clare Street in 1884. Amalgamation was an important trend in banks from the late nineteenth century and old-established Bristol banks such as Stuckeys disappeared in this period; the Capital & Counties Bank was taken over by Lloyds in 1918.

THE INDUSTRIAL SUBURBS

In 1850 nowhere in Bristol was far from the countryside: as late as 1874 two young boys playing near their home in St Pauls strayed as far as Horfield – then open countryside – and on a cold night Archie Walters, the elder of the two, died of exposure. Within twenty years rows of neat little terraced housing had completely transformed this scene, rapidly encroaching upon the Horfield countryside. In virtually every direction from the the centre, nurseries and farms were engulfed by new housing to accommodate Bristol's expanding population. By the early 1900s it was possible to travel for several miles from the centre before encountering open country. As in other cities, the new suburbs were socially differentiated with fashionable, residential suburbs in the west and areas of mainly working-class housing – the industrial suburbs – developing to the north, east and south.

Until the 1850s most of Bristol's working population lived in the old city, especially in St Philips, Redcliff and Temple where much industry was located; but as the old crowded courts and streets were converted to industrial and commercial use, the population of the inner city declined. Rows of small houses spread south in Bedminster and immediately east of the centre, stimulated by the arrival of the railway at Temple Meads. The opening of the Great Western Cotton mill was largely responsible for the suburban development of Barton Hill, and the growth of the collieries in Easton caused development there. St Philip's Marsh, an island between the Feeder Canal and the southward loop of the Avon, grew from the 1850s, creating a grid-iron of streets of red brick terraces, churches and chapels, corner shops and spit-and-sawdust public houses like the Victoria of 1873 – known affectionately to islanders as the 'Pig and Whistle'. In 1874 the Marsh was described as 'a gloomy vale enshrouded in almost perpetual smoke . . . home of the manure factories, bone crushing mills, knacker yards, horse flesh boiling factories and works in which the manufacture of chemical products throws off nauseous gases'. This was the archetypal industrial suburb with a working population tied closely to local industry: in 1871 Victoria Terrace in the Marsh (see page 120) was home to several labourers working in the neighbouring brickyards and potteries – including oven men and saggar makers; the terrace also housed a railway porter, a basket maker, a horse slaughterer and labourers working in the gas works and oil mills. The streets close to the engine sheds and Temple Meads station were full of engine drivers and other railway workers, whilst concentrations of coal miners were found in parts of Bedminster and Easton: in 1891 West Street in Bedminster, for example, had more colliers than any other occupation, although there were many general labourers and wives working as laundresses. Following the arrival of W.D. & H.O. Wills in Bedminster in 1886 many jobs were created in the area in the tobacco industry, and between 1851 and 1901 the population of Bedminster rose from 19,424 to 70,107.

Most of the housing consisted of terraced rows. Although no longer fashionable, the terrace remained the speculative builder's answer to the demand for cheap urban housing until the early 1900s. Cheap on land, materials and largely devoid of ornament, those built until the late 1870s were usually plain fronted with a parapet hiding a low roof supported against an extension of the party walls, which saved on roof timber. All Bristol's terraces were through houses with a rear back yard; there were no back-to-backs as in many northern towns, but the smaller house often lacked a through hall and opened straight on to the pavement. A superior plan incorporated a two-storey extension at the rear which provided space for a back kitchen, WC and coal shed as well as more bedroom space. The better quality house had a through passage which, in imitation of larger houses, promoted greater differentiation of room use: the front parlour was usually kept for best – a room for show facing the street – whilst the family lived in the back room or 'kitchen', separate from the back kitchen which housed the cooking range and washing copper.

As the suburbs grew they acquired their own distinctive character. The rows of terraced houses were followed by churches and chapels: new parishes were created – often supported by substantial middle-class aid to further religion amongst the labouring classes and help improve standards of moral behaviour. St Silas's, a new parish church for St Philip's Marsh, on the Feeder Road, was consecrated in 1867, and others followed in Bedminster and in the eastern suburbs. Many Nonconformist chapels were also built and by the early 1900s there were several Salvation Army and YMCA halls in the poorer districts. All the religious organisations aimed to reduce drunkenness amongst the working classes. In the mid-nineteenth century beer was the drink of working men and public houses were an important part of the working-class environment. John Latimer, the Bristol historian, reckoned that the number of inns, taverns and beer shops in the whole of Bristol rose from 650 in 1840 to about 1,250 in 1870, and the majority were to be found either in the old city or in the industrial suburbs. Some were named after local industries: the Mechanics Arms, for example, the Forgeman's Arms and the Colliery Tavern. However, writing in

1887, John Latimer remarked on the improved 'social habits' of the working classes since the mid-nineteenth century. The temperance movements and the churches may have had some success in reducing alcohol consumption; certainly the example of James Cox on page 98 is a striking story of the conversion of one rough, hard drinking individual with the help of the local Wesleyan chapel. The operation of the Licensing Act of 1872 fixed the closing time on Sundays at ten o'clock and was also instrumental in reducing the excessive number of beer shops, which had been able to obtain a licence at little cost. New leisure pursuits which developed towards the end of the nineteenth century also provided attractive alternatives to the public house. Nevertheless, public houses remained an integral part of social life in the industrial suburbs into the twentieth century, and in 1910 there were some thirty-three public houses in Bedminster alone.

The main thoroughfares, for example East Street, Bedminster, became important local shopping centres. Grocers' shops – frequently licensed to sell alcohol – grew rapidly in the late nineteenth century, often occupying a street corner amongst the rows of terraces; by the early 1900s there were also some twenty grocers' shops belonging to the Bristol Co-operative Society, founded in 1884. Fried fish shops became another distinguishing feature of the working-class districts in the late nineteenth century providing cheap nutritional food. In 1905, the first year they were listed separately in local directories, there were seventy-four fried fish dealers in Bristol, all located in the poorer districts, and five years later their number had increased to 126.

Other facilities were gradually added to the industrial suburbs. Schools were provided by the School Board established by the 1870 Education Act, and following the 1874 Public Libraries Act branch libraries were soon established in St Philips and Bedminster. Parks were created providing space for sport and leisure. The industrial suburbs, in effect, became self-contained communities. Bedminster, in particular, saw itself as a town within a city, a place apart, which by the time of the First World War was important enough to have its own music halls and cinemas.

The tramway was another essential part of Bristol's industrial suburbs from 1875 and stimulated development further afield. Before the advent of trams the areas of working-class housing were still close to the centre, but once tramlines were laid on major routes out of the city large-scale urban development began in Horfield, Bishopston, Eastville, Stapleton and Fishponds. Building was delayed by a slump in the early 1880s, but resumed before the end of the decade and continued at a furious pace through the 1890s, a decade which also saw extensive development south of the Avon in St Annes, Totterdown, Southville and in the new suburb growing up around the docks at Avonmouth.

The terraces of this second major phase of development are easily distinguished from those built before 1880. The most striking difference is in the façade, which frequently incorporates a bay window, either one or two storey, whilst the roof is integrated into the overall design projecting on eaves and pitched more steeply instead of being hidden behind a low parapet. There were many subtle variations in the size and quality of the terrace, and whilst these were evident before 1880 they became more pronounced from the late 1880s. The quality of the front elevation and also of the internal decorations – the amount of moulded plasterwork, joinery and the quality of the fireplaces – expressed the social hierarchy within the working class between the higher paid artisans and the unskilled labourer. And although Bishopston, Horfield, Southville and other areas may have lacked the exclusiveness of the affluent suburbs, they began to acquire a residential character of their own. By 1900 the distinction between the industrial and fashionable suburbs was less precise than it had been in 1875. Whilst the terraced houses built at the end of the nineteenth century may have been monotonous they were controlled by housing by-laws, which ensured that basic standards of construction, sanitation and adequate space, front and back, were maintained. The larger houses were villas within a terrace – many had names following the fashions of the affluent suburbs – and with their solid, respectable exteriors provided homes worthy of the upwardly mobile artisan class.

William Bailey, haulier, Feeder Road, St Philip's Marsh, between 1904 and 1909. The Stone Manure Company, horse slaughterers and manure manufacturers from 1888, was at the top of Arthur Street (left) on the Feeder Road. The company belonged to Arthur Stone who built twelve houses in Arthur Street in 1896–7. William Bailey, who is presumably seen standing here by his wagon, is recorded as a haulier in Feeder Road from 1904 to 1909.

Children pose for the camera outside Parker's corner shop, St Philip's Marsh, *c.* 1906. One or two are poorly dressed with open-toed shoes and ill-fitting clothes, but most appear to be wearing their best – the boys in Eton collars and one little boy on the right in a sailor's top; possibly the occasion was an outing to Weston-super-Mare.

Frederick Parker ran this shop on the corner of Short Street and Victoria Terrace between 1895 and 1910. Corner shops were an important part of working-class suburbs and provided for most of the regular needs of the local population. They were stocked with a wide range of goods usually mixed in glorious disarray, like the exterior advertisements here which mix foodstuffs and hardware: condensed milk – a cheap alternative to fresh milk was first introduced in the 1860s and the Swiss company Nestlé founded in 1904; cocoa and chocolate were no longer luxury goods and Fry's like the other major producers made cheap products within reach of the working-class family; a tin of Peak Frean's biscuits can also be glimpsed inside the door; Parker was also licensed to sell tobacco. Corner shops also supplied a wide range of hardware including soap (Hudson's were a Midlands firm), starch, laundry blue, candles, matches and black-lead; here we see Henkel's bleach advertised in the doorway and boxes of Lions black-lead used to polish grates and the kitchen range piled high inside the shop window.

St Philip's Marsh was a close-knit community broken up in the 1950s when the housing was cleared to make way for an industrial estate. In 1996 the site of the corner shop was an untidy scrap of wasteland bounded by barbed wire.

Upton Road, Southville, *c.* 1915. Many of the houses in this road were built between 1896 and 1898 but were overshadowed by Wills's factory number eight in Raleigh Road, which was originally used to pack tinned tobacco and snuff.

East Street, Bedminster, *c.* 1912. This busy shopping street is dominated by the imposing Gothic-style factory of W.D. & H.O. Wills, built of deep red Cattybrook bricks in 1886 and designed by Sir Frank Wills. The covered cart outside the factory belongs to Mardon Son & Hall, printers and packagers who had joined Wills in the Imperial Tobacco Group in 1902.

Corner of Brook Street and St John's Road, Bedminster, c.1919. A scene reminiscent of an urban landscape by the painter L.S. Lowry as workers – mainly women – emerge from the Wills factory on St John's Road. Most seem unaware of the photographer although some of the children have seen him, such as the girl in the centre foreground shading her eyes from the bright midday sun as she faces the camera. Her left shoe is open toed.

The close proximity of terraced houses and corner shop to the tobacco factory typify the environment of the industrial suburbs. The houses with their plain fronts and parapet roofs date from the 1870s and are typical of those built in the third quarter of the nineteenth century. The lantern of the gas lamp on the left has been painted blue – a First World War air raid precaution, introduced in March 1915, although there were no attacks on Bristol from German aircraft. The taller block on the right was a bonded warehouse built for the Imperial Tobacco Company by Cowlins in 1914. All the buildings on the right have now gone and the site is now occupied by an Asda supermarket; however, the shop on the corner survives.

St Luke's Road, Bedminster, *c.* 1910. This road bounding Victoria Park was developed from the late 1860s and through the 1870s with plain fronted terraced houses of a type common throughout Bristol's industrial suburbs.

George King and family outside their Bedminster home, 131 Whitehouse Lane, *c.* 1910. This plain brick terraced house which backed on to the railway line from Temple Meads was one of thirty-two houses erected by a builder called Adams in 1896; they were extremely small and basic with a parlour, kitchen and tiny scullery crammed into the main block, three small bedrooms upstairs but no rear extension, except for a small structure housing the WC.

Nutgrove Avenue, Victoria Park, Bedminster, *c.* 1910. In contrast to George King's small dwelling, opposite below, in Whitehouse Lane, just across the main railway line and Victoria Park were these substantial terraced houses in Nutgrove Avenue, also built in about 1896.

Victoria Park, *c.* 1910. In 1888 land at Windmill Hill, Bedminster, was purchased from Sir Greville Smyth and 51 acres were turned into a public park. Like many Victorian public parks it had a bandstand and a popular feature – a redundant cannon, this one a rifled muzzle loading gun probably dating from the 1870s. The industrial setting of the park is emphasised by the chimneys of Wills's factories in the background.

Badminton Road, St Agnes, *c.* 1910. Substantial terraced houses with two-storey bays in Badminton Road built in the mid-1890s belie the reputation of this district for poverty; Clifton College supported a mission here. The tower of St Agnes's parish church, consecrated in 1886, can be seen in the background.

Committee of the Loyal St George Sick Benefit Society, 1903. Voluntary associations such as this were common in working-class communities before the emergence of the welfare state. Standing from left: C.A. Broome, J. Walker, G. Johns, H. Stokes, T. Calloway, R. Dempsey, H. Mann, E. Mayo; seated: H.J. Silcocks, P. McCarthy, C.J. Strawbridge, D. Daley; front: R. Pearse, W.J. Headford, G. Thompson.

Maple Road, Horfield, *c.* 1894. Builders take a break from building a terraced row in Maple Road beween Thornleigh Road and Ash Road. The roofs are on but some wooden scaffolding remains and the joiner is still required to fit the sash windows and doors, and there is plenty of work for the plasterers seen here. The man standing confidently in the centre and the only one wearing collar and tie may be Walter Collison, the builder and contractor who submitted the plans for these houses to the Horfield Local Board (responsible for imposing statutory building regulations) on 19 April 1894.

Between 1892 and 1894 Collison, of 8 Church Road, Horfield, was responsible for the construction of some forty-eight terraced houses at the Gloucester Road end of Maple Road and a large number of similar houses in Thornleigh Road, Ash Road and Elm Road. A 'for sale' sign is visible in the photograph and Collison, who, like most small builders had probably taken out a loan to finance the speculation, was no doubt counting on a speedy sale. The houses were often bought by shopkeepers and other small tradesmen who let them out to tenants.

Collison's houses followed a typical plan, with a parlour and living room on the ground floor and a kitchen, coal shed and WC in a rear extension; upstairs there were three bedrooms but no bathroom. His houses had attractive façades of blue-grey Pennant sandstone and ashlar window and door surrounds. The bays had projecting roofs surmounted by terracotta finials. Sadly, many of the houses have been altered and have lost some of their original features, but they survive over a hundred years later and provide roomier and more attractive accommodation than much twentieth-century mass housing.

Ashton swing bridge, *c.* 1910. Opened in 1906, this bridge spanning the New Cut was a complicated and expensive structure: it was both a road and railway bridge and also a swing bridge which could open to allow tall masted vessels to pass. Operations were controlled from a cabin erected over the bridge.

Ashton Gate Toll House, Ashton Gate, *c.* 1910. This was one of fifteen turnpike gates in Bristol in the 1850s; the turnpike trustees levied tolls from road users to maintain the road. The last of the turnpikes was removed in 1867 and the roads came under municipal control. Most of the toll houses were demolished but this one survived and gave its name to the district, and, of course, a well-known football ground!

Timber trolley of Frederick Niblett, hauliers of 42 Parson Street from about 1909 to 1923, outside the White Horse, West Street, Bedminster, *c.* 1910. The empty timber trolley may be returning to Parson Street having off-loaded a delivery of timber to one of the timber dealers and saw mills then in business further up West Street. The driver is Tom Reeves, who is wearing clogs, gaiters and a woollen jersey under his jacket. Tram lines cross the foreground of the cobbled street, which shows signs of horse droppings, a common sight on roads when horses were the main source of motive power.

Public houses were an essential part of the working-class suburb; the White Horse, one of several pubs along West Street, was an old-established public house, listed in Mathews 1793–4 Bristol Directory. It was clearly given a major rebuild in the early 1900s. Advertisements for whiskies and port are displayed in the window and hanging by the entrance is a sign of the National Telephone Company, which provided by far the majority of Britain's telephones and exchanges from 1880 until 1911 when the GPO took over the entire telephone network. The outward appearance of the pub is little changed today.

Chessel Street on the right was developed between about 1899 and 1903, and contains typical small terraced houses of the period.

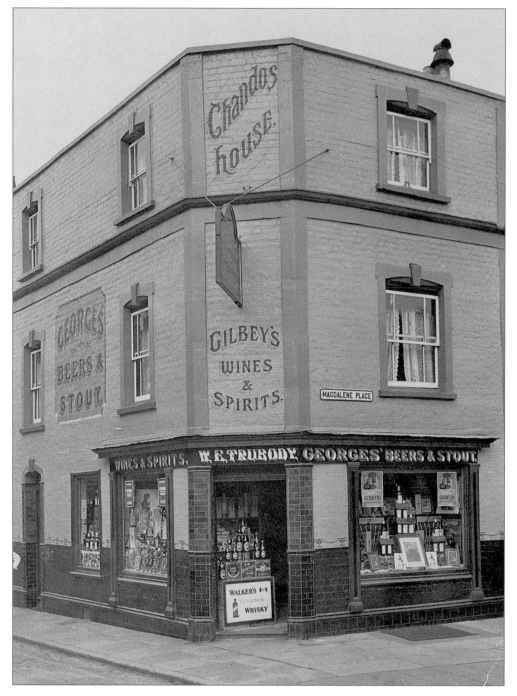

William Ernest Trubody's corner shop, 64 Magdelene Place, Lower Ashley Road, *c*. 1910. An attractive shop exterior with painted brickwork, a decorative frieze, tiles (probably dark green) around the door and shaded signwriting above for W.E. Trubody, grocer licensed to sell alcoholic beverages. Georges beers are also prominently advertised and some bottled beers can be seen displayed in the doorway. In 1850 there were 279 grocers and tea dealers in Bristol; by 1906, when Trubody entered business, the figure had risen to 881 including the co-operative shops. Trubody ran the shop until 1939.

Mr Brown's shop, Easton, *c.* 1905. The interior of a grocer's shop with typical fittings of the time: a long straight wooden counter and hanging shelves which are stacked with different varieties of Peak Frean's 'celebrated biscuits' and a box of Fry's chocolate creams. The gas light above the counter consists of simple flat flame burners which did not require glass chimneys or shades (see also the kitchen on page 111).

Bath Road, Bristol.

The industrial suburbs, east: Bath Road looking towards Brislington, *c.* 1910. Between the houses lining Bath Street, terraced houses of the 1890s in Upper Street, Totterdown, hang precariously from their steep hillside site above the Turnpike Inn, formerly the toll house on the turnpike road to Bath.

Railway Station, Shirehampton. 1822

The industrial suburbs, west: Shirehampton station, *c.* 1912. The area west of the city was mainly associated with the affluent suburbs but Bristol acquired a small industrial suburb further west when Shirehampton and Avonmouth became part of Bristol, following the extension of the city boundaries in 1904. The railway opened in 1865.

THE FASHIONABLE SUBURBS

As working-class suburbs spread into the fields south and east of the old city, wealthy solicitors, accountants, mortgage brokers, insurance agents, doctors, merchants and manufacturers established their homes in Clifton, Cotham and Redland, and further afield in Sneyd Park, Stoke Bishop and Leigh Woods. There were exceptions: Knowle enjoyed a brief spell as a desirable area, there were some middle-class villas in Bedminster and enclaves of working-class terraced housing could be found in the affluent suburbs. Nevertheless, the general picture remains of quiet suburbs of substantial houses, an environment that embodied middle-class values and aspirations.

The fashionable suburbs represented the complete separation of work and home. In the eighteenth century industrialists and tradesmen usually lived over their working premises, but from the early nineteenth century affluent citizens withdrew from the city to Kingsdown and to Clifton. Secure from the noise, dirt and immorality of city life, the rising middle classes could lead respectable lives in their well-built villas in leafy roads with respectable names. And the road names were important, as they helped to create the right atmosphere: 'street' was not acceptable – it conveyed too much of the city; and in Clifton Gallows Acre Lane was renamed Pembroke Road. Lanes, after all, were rural, muddy and inconvenient and public executions were (from the 1860s) a thing of the past.

House names were important too: Albion, Richmond and Belmont Villa were solid and respectable and added to the uniqueness of the family home. Until the mid-nineteenth century the fashionable home in Bristol was typically within a terrace where the individual dwelling was subsumed within the identity of the whole block. They usually occupied commanding sites close to the street, square or pavement, and were public and very showy. The Victorian middle classes, in contrast, desired separateness and seclusion, and so from the mid-nineteenth century the fashionable terrace fell from favour and was replaced by the large detached or semi-detached villa. These were usually set back from the road offering greater privacy, and for the first time gardens became an important part of the urban home environment.

Separateness and individuality were also achieved through the style of the house. There were different styles to choose from: Grecian, Gothic and Tudor, but most popular was the Italianate style which was adopted for many large houses built in the 1860s. Typically, the large Victorian villa boasted large bay windows which not only added to the light and spaciousness of the interior but emphasised the importance of the window in the façade. Details could vary: window openings of carved Bath stone or moulded terracotta provided points of individual interest to each house. Gabled roofs were also popular and again decorative barge boards provided opportunities for individual treatment. Some of the houses were faced in ashlar like the detached houses in Victoria Square, Clifton, whilst others were rendered; but the finest and largest in parts of Clifton, Redland and Sneyd Park were built of grey or pink Pennant sandstone, which contrasted well with the light coloured Bath stone used for corners, door and window surrounds.

These houses were large – twelve rooms or more; families were generally larger but space was also required for the servants. Keeping servants was the distinguishing feature of being middle class: some of the grandest establishments in Royal York Crescent had as many as six including a butler; two servants – a cook and a parlour maid – was common; and in 1881 a modest row of houses in Auburn Road, Redland (the homes of a retired ship master, a commercial clerk, a minister, a solicitor's clerk and three young unmarried sisters), each had one resident female servant. The principal rooms of the house were usually situated over a basement which contained a suite of service rooms, separate, physically and socially, from the family areas. Plans of 1862 for villas in Tyndalls Park show stairs leading to a basement kitchen, scullery, wine cellar, pantry and house keeper's room.

The presence of servants and people in supporting trades – laundresses, dressmakers and shopkeepers – could account for a considerable percentage of the residents in an affluent suburb. In his study of Clifton, Donald Jones has shown that of a random sample of 709 houses over 47 per cent of the population comprised servants and others in service industries. Nevertheless, their presence did not affect the exclusiveness of the fashionable suburbs. In 1878 one Cliftonian could write to the *Bristol Mercury*, 'Poor people do not walk about on Clifton streets', adding, 'We have nothing common or unclean amongst us'. He and others wanted to keep it that way and objected strongly to the proposal to extend the 'disgusting tramway' into Clifton. The tram, they believed, threatened to bring the 'nasty, low inhabitants of Bristol' up into Clifton where they would encourage jerry building, depress property values and tempt residents to shop in Bristol to the detriment of local traders.

The extension to the tramway was, indeed, rejected by the City Corporation and Clifton remained free from the threat of lower-class immigrants. Clifton, however, was never a typical middle-class suburb; it owed its rise as a fashionable area to the nearby Hotwells, which had attracted wealthy people seeking a cure from the Hotwell water since the seventeenth century. Hotwells enjoyed its heyday in the mid-eighteenth century, but its popularity was already waning in the 1790s when speculative builders began the construction of large terraces overlooking the Gorge. From the heights above the Avon the residents of Clifton enjoyed life in an exclusive suburb with fresh air, clean water and pleasant views over to Somerset. Clifton always remained a place apart – even following its absorption into Bristol in 1835. There were stately terraces with graceful iron verandas, expensive shops in elegant streets, beautiful churches, public schools and good hotels, but no red brick public houses, no fried fish shops, few corner shops – and no trams. There was a strong upper middle-class, even aristocratic, air to Clifton; it was home to members of the gentry, senior Anglican Clergy, admirals, army officers, professional and literary people and, according to 'Lesser Columbus' in 1893, 'Unmarried ladies of matured, single experience'.

Clifton, Cotham and Redland grew rapidly after 1850 fuelled by the optimism of speculative builders. Within a year of the opening of the Clifton Suspension Bridge to road traffic in 1865 building lots were being advertised in Leigh Woods, and in the 1870s Alpenfels, the Swiss chalet-style house was built near the bridge for Francis Fox, the Chief Engineer of the Bristol and Exeter Railway. The expansion of Redland proceeded at a dramatic pace; in 1867 it was reported that 300 houses were being built in one scheme alone. From the 1870s the development crossed the Downs – secured as a public park by Act of Parliament in 1862 – to Sneyd Park and Stoke Bishop and, from the 1890s, Henleaze. The search for the fashionable home was taking the affluent Bristolian ever further from the old city.

Hotwells, 1850s. The old Hotwell house, dating from about 1696, was removed in 1822 to allow the construction of Bridge Valley Road. A new pump room was constructed, but this did not stop the decline of the spring and it was demolished when Hotwell Point was removed in 1868.

Hotwells pump, *c.* 1880. Following the removal of Hotwell Point on the Avon to improve navigation in 1868, the hot spring at the Hotwell was lost, and following local complaints this ornate pump was erected in 1877 within a cavern in the nearby cliff; however, it was doubted if this supplied the true spring water, and even if it did the distance between the source and the pump caused the water to lose its characteristic temperature.

Clifton Suspension Bridge, 1850s. For some ten years the famous suspension bridge designed by Isambard Kingdom Brunel (1806–59) lay abandoned. The two piers stood folorn and unloved – they were considered an eyesore – and the Clifton Improvement Society even proposed their demolition! Work had begun in 1831 on the Clifton side, but it was the construction of the massive abutment on the Somerset bank which exhausted the funds, and work was abandoned in 1853.

Clifton Suspension Bridge, 1875. A new company was formed to complete the bridge in 1861 and work resumed the following year. The bridge was finally opened amidst huge celebrations on 8 December 1864. Brunel, however, did not live to witness the event: he had died in 1859 and never saw completed what is generally regarded as his masterpiece. The bridge was opened to vehicular traffic on 23 January 1865 and almost immediately stimulated the development of Leigh Woods on the Somerset side as an exclusive suburb.

Sion Hill, Clifton, 1870s. Elegant houses with first-floor iron balconies, typical of late Georgian Clifton, overlook the Avon Gorge and exude the air of a Regency seaside town. The St Vincent's Rock Hotel in the foreground was opened in October 1868 in the former pump room of the Sion spring, established in 1811; by 1845 the spring was also supplying piped water to 304 dwellings in the neighbourhood.

Grand Spa Hotel, Clifton, *c.* 1910. Typical late Victorian street furniture in Sion Hill includes, on the right, a cabman's rest, introduced in Bristol in 1874; an electric arc street lamp, introduced in Clifton from 1898; and a letter box, first appearing in Bristol in 1856: by 1908 there were 461. This one dates from 1879–87, and survives in 1996. The hotel was opened in March 1898 in a final attempt to re-establish the Hotwell.

The Royal Parade, Queens Road, Clifton, 1870s. A commercial terrace containing fashionable shops, designed by Foster & Wood in the 1850s.

George V visiting the Victoria Assembly Rooms, 1913. Designed by Charles Dyer and built in 1839–41, this impressive Grecian building served as a concert hall and meetings room for Clifton. George V unveiled the bronze statue of his father, Edward VII, by Henry Poole, surrounded by fountains on 4 July 1913. Here the King is seen saluting the crowd, which includes several women holding umbrellas to ward off the sun.

Regent Street, *c.* 1915. This was the main Victorian shopping street of Clifton. The W.H. Smith shop in Regent Street, opened in 1905, was the first in Bristol outside Temple Meads station.

Whiteladies Road, *c.* 1910. Whiteladies Road was subject to various street improvements in the second half of the nineteenth century, including road widening and better drainage. The tram lines were laid in 1874 and opened as far as Black Boy Hill on 9 August 1875; an extension to Westbury-on-Trym was opened on 23 October 1908.

Albert Hallet, confectioner, Black Boy Hill, Redland, 1899. Advertisements for Fry's chocolates adorn the windows of this shop, which was in business here from about 1878 until about 1917.

Vyvyan Terrace, Clifton, *c.* 1910. Named after Sir Richard Vyvyan (1800–79), a Conservative Member of Parliament for Bristol in the 1830s, this impressive Ionic-pillared terrace was built in the early 1840s and included the homes of members of Bristol's social elite throughout the rest of the nineteenth century.

Royal Promenade, Victoria Square, Clifton, *c.* 1910. Begun in the 1830s, Victoria Square contains some of the finest large terraces in Clifton, and this view shows Royal Promenade – a palatial group of fifteen houses designed by James Foster & Son in 1837 but not completed until the early 1850s. The square was not finished until 1874 by which time the popularity of the fashionable terraced house had waned.

Victoria Square, Clifton, 1850s. A magnificent four lantern gas lamp dominates the north-east side of the square; a similar lamp stood by the Victoria Assembly Rooms but these were exceptional: Bristol was one of the worst lit cities in the country in 1850. The effectiveness of this lamp would have been limited by mid-Victorian gas technology – the simple flat flame burners produced a poor light. Lansdown Terrace, built in 1835, is to the right, Royal Promenade in the distance.

Upper Belgrave Road, Durdham Down, *c.* 1910. These large Italianate villas are typical of those built in Clifton from the 1850s to replace the large terrace as the fashionable home for the affluent residents in Clifton, Cotham and Redland. Joseph Storrs Fry lived at number 16 until his death in 1913.

Roseneath, 6 West Park, Cotham, *c.* 1910. This was the home of Andrew and Frances Brewer and their children (see page 78), and is typical of the villa homes built in Clifton, Cotham and Redland in the third quarter of the nineteenth century. (A. Brewer)

View across the back gardens of houses in Rockleaze, Sneyd Park, *c.* 1875. Gardens became an important part of the Victorian middle-class suburb.

Ivywell Road, Sneyd Park, *c.* 1912. These substantial stone villas of the 1870s, each one clearly different from its neighbour, are set back from the road.

John Herbert Brewer (born 8 January 1913) with his monthly nurse, who stayed with the mother and child for one month after the baby's birth at 6 West Park, Cotham. His parents were Andrew Brewer (1870–1935), an accountant who worked in Bath, and Frances Edith Brewer (1870–1931). (A. Brewer)

Frances Harriet (born 1900) and Dorothy Edith (born 1902) on a toy horse in the back garden of 6 West Park, Cotham, c. 1906. (A.Brewer)

An Edwardian doll party at 6 West Park, Cotham, *c.* 1910. (A. Brewer)

Redland Bank, Redland Hill, *c.* 1875. This was home to John Lucas and his son Charles, African merchants; in 1871 four daughters were also resident and there were two servants, a domestic cook and a parlour maid. The house was demolished in 1961.

Maidservant laundering clothes, Redland Villa, home of the Feddon family, *c.* 1858. The servant population of the fashionable suburbs formed a substantial percentage of the total. In this carefully arranged composition the girl is posed scrubbing the clothes in a wooden wash tub – washing machines were virtually unknown in the 1850s. A hot water can sits in the foreground.

A HOME IN THE COUNTRY

Wealthy Bristolians had been moving out of the congested and polluted city for a quieter, more spacious country home since the eighteenth century, and the large houses in the countryside surrounding the city were a mix of the homes of rural landowners (the gentry), like the Sampsons of Henbury Manor, and those of wealthy Bristol industrialists. The Harfords, Bristol bankers and industrialists, had moved to the Blaise Castle Estate, Henbury, in 1789. Charles Thomas, soap and candle maker, whose factory poured smoke into the sky above Broad Plain lived in the peaceful surroundings of Pitch and Pay Lane in Stoke Bishop. The Grove, a late eighteenth-century house set in extensive grounds at Brislington, was the home of the Ricketts family, Bristol glass manufacturers until 1862; from 1878 until 1899 it was occupied by Richard Cripps, an importer of Italian marble at Redcliff Wharf. After 1900 urbanisation encroached upon Brislington and the house lost its rural character. The search for a home firmly in the country could take affluent Bristolians even further from the city. Lord Winterstoke (W.H. Wills) acquired a country estate at Blagdon, Somerset, where he assumed the identity of a typical large country landowner, developing a model farm and dairy.

Gentlemen landowners like the Sampsons in Henbury – the local squires – were owners of farms which were held on fixed terms by tenant farmers. There were many farms, smallholdings and market gardens around Bristol. There were sixteen farms alone in Brislington – and others in Horfield, Henbury and elsewhere. Dairying was a major occupation: milk and vegetables were sold to suppliers in the city and some farmers also supplied straw and hay for the city's large population of working horses. Farm labourers either lived in cottages on the farms or in the neighbouring village, and whilst the cottage exterior often suggested an idyllic existence those who took the trouble to look inside often found cramped and insanitary conditions every bit as bad as the city slums.

Shooting at Lawrence Weston Farm, Boxing Day, 1914. Clemant Hignell, tenant farmer of Lawrence Weston Farm from 1908 to 1917, is second from left in the bowler hat.

Westmorland Farm, Henbury, *c.* 1920. This 146 acre farm was let annually from the Sampsons of Henbury Manor. The farm supplied the stables of the Mansion House, residence of the Lord Mayor, with hay and straw; cider, cheese and bread were produced in the farmhouse until the 1930s.

Cottage at Coombe Dingle, *c*. 1875. An attractive winter scene with snow on the ground and a wisp of smoke rising from the chimney. Free from the dense housing of the old city and the new industrial suburbs, rural cottages could appear to offer an idyllic home environment: the reality was that many farm labourers' cottages were as overcrowded and insanitary as any urban slum.

The drawing room at Blaise Castle, *c*. 1900. Blaise Castle, designed by Robert Milne, was built as a summer house in about 1768 for Thomas Farr, owner of the Blaise Castle Estate from 1762 to 1778. For a short period after the First World War it provided unusual accommodation for C. Castell, a woodman on the estate, as no other cottages were available; he and his wife lived in the ground floor kitchen and used one of the towers as a bedroom.

Blaise Castle House, Henbury, 1870s. The house was built in 1796 by John Harford, a wealthy Bristol banker and merchant who had previously lived close to his business interests in Brunswick Square; this view from the south-east shows, from left, the original house designed by William Paty, the Ionic colonnade of Charles Cockerell's picture gallery built in 1832–33 and, right foreground, the elegant conservatory designed by John Nash in about 1806. The parkland, several hundred acres in extent, can be glimpsed in the background.

Mary Harford with her family at Blaise Castle House, 11 June 1909. This was Mary Harford's seventieth birthday and she is seen gathered with members of her family in front of a structure – now demolished – which linked the picture room with the conservatory; she is sixth from left, a tiny figure holding a posy of flowers, seated next to her son Frederick and his wife. Within a few years of Mary Harford's death in 1919, the Harfords had sold the estate to the City Council for recreational use.

Blaise Hamlet, Henbury, *c*. 1900. Designed by John Nash, the fashionable Regency architect, and George Repton in the Picturesque style, Blaise Hamlet was built between 1810 and 1811 by John Harford, owner of the Blaise Castle Estate, to provide homes for his estate workers and retired servants. The nine cottages were arranged informally around a village green; each one was different from its neighbour although all had towering chimneys of moulded brickwork. The result was one of the finest examples of picturesque cottage construction anywhere. The hamlet was soon established as a local Bristol beauty spot and was a popular subject with Victorian and Edwardian photographers.

Albert and Martha Jefferies outside their home, Circular Cottage, Blaise Hamlet, *c*. 1900. Albert Jefferies worked as a carter for the Harfords. Although the cottages were small they provided better accommodation than the average nineteenth-century farm labourer's cottage; each one had an oven, washing copper and privy.

A wealthy Bristol merchant in his country home: Richard Cripps with members of his family relaxing in the garden of The Grove, Wick Road, Brislington, *c.* 1880. Richard Cripps was an Italian marble importer with commercial premises on Redcliff Back.

The Grove, Wick Road, Brislington, *c.* 1880. This eighteenth-century house was the home of the Ricketts family, Bristol glass manufacturers from the late eighteenth century until 1862. From 1878 until 1899 it was occupied by Richard Cripps (left) and his family. The house survives as flats but the extensive gardens were built over with houses in Grove Park Road, Pendennis Park, Montrose Park and Bristol Hill.

RELIGION

A national religious census carried out in 1851 revealed that church attendance in Bristol was higher than in other cities of comparable size: roughly a third of the population regularly attended a church or chapel and this figure was being maintained thirty years later when the *Western Daily Press* carried out a local survey. Religion, therefore, was a major part of life in Victorian and Edwardian Bristol and through its response to the social problems created by the city's expansion exerted a strong influence on the city's development.

The 1851 census confirmed the supremacy of the Church of England which claimed 45.5 per cent of churchgoers and dominated the city's political life: 80 per cent of city councillors were Anglican. Nevertheless, the census also showed that the combined church attendance of the various Nonconformist denominations and the Roman Catholic Church accounted for 55.5 per cent of the total. Bristol had a long association with Protestant Dissent dating from the mid-seventeenth century, and was also closely associated with the origins of Methodism: John Wesley had established his first chapel in Bristol in 1739.

There were enormous differences – social as much as doctrinal – between the Established Church and some of the more extreme evangelical sects such as the Primitive Methodists. The parish church of St Andrew, Clifton, for example, was not a church for the poor man: 'he has no business there', wrote an observer in the 1840s, 'in that atmosphere of *eau de cologne* and *bouquet de la Reine*.' St Andrew's and a Wesleyan chapel in Bedminster or Easton attended by the labouring poor were worlds apart, but the second half of the nineteenth century saw some lowering of barriers between denominations. Dissenting Protestants had gained full political rights in 1828 and Roman Catholics in 1829 (Jews had to wait until 1858), and many wealthy and influential citizens, notably members of the Wills and Fry families were Nonconformist and played a leading part in municipal affairs.

All denominations were united in their mission to bring religion, temperance, cleanliness and improved standards of public behaviour to the urban masses. Horace Mann, the chief statistician of the 1851 census, stated that the 'labouring myriads, the masses of our working population . . . are but seldom seen in our religious congregations'. Voluntary organisations, closely supported by the city's clergy, which sought to 'civilise' the poor by distributing religious tracts and preaching, were active through the nineteenth century. There were also a number of temperance organisations such as the Bristol Temperance Society and the Band of Hope Union, which made the removal of drunkenness – seen by Victorian reformers as one of the great evils of the working class – their objective. Temperance hotels and coffee taverns were sponsored by the movements in an effort to attract the working class away from the beer houses. The Young Men's Christian Association, a Nonconformist organisation, was established in the city in 1853 with the objective of self improvement for young men, and once it began organising sports facilities its success was assured. Branches of the YMCA were opened in Bedminster, Easton, Fishponds, Hotwells and Totterdown.

Church leaders were concerned at the acute shortage, or absence altogether, of places of worship in the new suburbs. Church extension commissions helped to identify the areas where they were most needed, and between 1850 and 1919 the number of places of religious worship of all denominations increased from 83 to about 260. The number of Church of England places of worship more than doubled over this period. Clifton acquired several new Anglican churches after 1850: St Paul's in 1853 and then two in the 1860s – All Saints', Pembroke Road and Emmanuel, Guthrie Road – built as a response to the development of Clifton then taking place towards the Downs; St Anselm's, Whately Road, followed in 1897. New churches were also added in the affluent areas of Stoke Bishop and Leigh Woods. In Bedminster the parish church of St John's, a small seventeenth-century structure, was replaced by a new larger church in 1855, and by 1910 another nine Anglican churches had been built in Bedminster, Totterdown and Knowle. Several new churches had been opened in the new eastern industrial suburbs in the 1840s – in Barton Hill, Easton and Montpelier – and between 1850 and 1909 another fourteen were added. St Werburgh's, one of the old city churches, was relocated from Corn Street to Mina Road in 1879. St Philip's Marsh acquired a parish church, St Silas's, in 1867, and a church was opened in Avonmouth in 1893. St Agnes's, Newfoundland Road, consecrated in 1886, cost £5,000, half of which was donated by Clifton College which had established a mission there in 1875. Several other churches in the centre and Clifton followed this example and adopted poor areas, carrying out missionary work and providing financial support for new churches: thus, St Paul's, Clifton, helped finance the building of St Michael and All Angels, Windmill Hill, in 1886.

The expansion of the Nonconformist denominations followed similar lines. The number of Baptist chapels in this period increased from seven to twenty-six and the affluent congregation of the Buckingham Baptist chapel in Clifton took on missionary work in Hotwells. Congregational church building had been vigorous in the mid-nineteenth century when Arley chapel, Cheltenham Road and Highbury chapel, Cotham were built, but lost momentum until the end of the century when an extension movement stimulated the building of new places of worship in Brislington, Bedminster, Henleaze and Avonmouth. Both the Baptists and the Congregationalists built new training colleges in Cotham in the early 1900s. The industrial suburbs, where the evangelical message of Methodism exerted a strong hold amongst the poor, also acquired many new chapels; by 1919 there were over sixty belonging to the various Methodist churches. The expansion of Roman Catholicism was slower, however, and in 1919 there were only ten churches besides a few convents in the city.

The building of new churches and the restoration of older churches was the visible manifestation of the energy of the various religious bodies in Victorian and Edwardian Bristol. Whilst providing for the religious needs of the growing population they were also built to enhance the physical environment. The public appeal for the restoration of St Mary Redcliffe, published in 1842, was intended to create 'a national monument of unequalled beauty'. New imposing churches were an important feature of the Victorian reworking of the city: new towers and spires appeared on the skyline, whilst in the poorer suburbs the small stone chapels with a traceried window facing the street provided welcome relief from the drab rows of terraces and factories. From the mid-nineteenth century Gothic came to be regarded as the only true Christian architecture, and after the mid-century swept alternative styles – Grecian and Italianate – to one side. The designs were mostly conceived as accurate representations of medieval ecclesiastical architecture: Buckingham Baptist chapel, designed by the local architect Richard Shackleton Pope, with its soaring pinnacles, sharply pointed blank arcading and rose window was a successful essay in the Continental High Gothic manner, and was generally admired upon its completion in 1847. Beautifully proportioned and carefully detailed designs in Early English and Decorated Gothic by John Norton, a London architect, were provided for the replacement church of St John's, Bedminster, St Mary Magdelene, Stoke Bishop, and Holy Trinity, Stapleton.

Norton also designed the spire added to Christ Church, Clifton, in 1859. Church spires were an important and conspicuous element of Victorian Gothic architecture. The replacement of the spire of St Mary Redcliffe, that 'splendid, heavenly pointing member', in the words of the 1842 appeal, was seen as the crowning glory of the restored church; it would bear comparison, it was confidently asserted, with some of the finest in Europe including Strasbourg, Salisbury and Norwich. Religion, aesthetics and civic pride became intertwined. The restoration and expansion of the Cathedral was a matter of practical expediency – the church was simply too small – but it was also of general concern that the city lacked a cathedral of sufficient grandeur, and so the appeal to enlarge the Cathedral and provide it with two west towers received support from leading Nonconformists as well as Anglicans in the city. Anglican churches, in particular, lacking a tower and especially a spire were seen to be incomplete: John Latimer, writing in 1887 of All Saints', Pembroke Road, Clifton, an ornate and massive structure by the London architect George Edmund Street, remarked that (lacking its tower and spire through want of funds), 'the church viewed from a distance, presents the appearance of a gigantic barn'. All Saints' eventually acquired a tower but two churches by John Norton, Emmanuel, Clifton, and St John's, Bedminster, never acquired a spire.

Church building was not simply a matter of show and prestige. Religion and particularly doctrinal issues were also important in deciding architectural details, and there were several major disputes which exposed some of the deep differences between the High and Low Church factions within the Church of England. In 1855 the erection of a richly sculptured reredos in the new church of St John's, Bedminster, created a storm of protest from Low Church clergy who saw it as 'papistical'. Some twenty years later a similar reaction was provoked during the restoration of the cathedral, when statues above the north porch were given cardinals' hats by the sculptor: Low Church supporters claimed they were an insult to Protestantism and the Dean, Gilbert Elliot, a prominent low churchman, had them torn down. Divisive tendencies persisted throughout the period. When a United Thanksgiving service to mark the end of the First World War was held in the Cathedral on 20 November 1918, some clergy protested against the participation of the Pastor of Highbury Congregational Church; making no apology, the Bishop replied that this was a united service for all Christians.

Nevertheless, the city now had an enlarged cathedral and the bishopric and diocese which had been split in 1836 was restored in 1897. Throughout the city, there were many new churches and chapels to cater for the spiritual needs of a city where religion remained an important force in shaping the future.

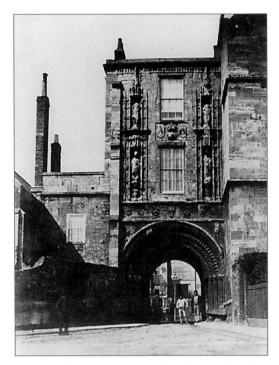

Abbey gateway, May 1858. The Augustinian Abbey, founded in 1140 by Robert Fitzharding, a prominent Bristol citizen was established as the cathedral in 1542 when the diocese of Bristol was formed. When the abbey was suppressed by Henry VIII in 1539 work was underway on rebuilding the nave but this was stopped and until the mid-nineteenth century the cathedral could only accommodate a congregation of 300. In 1836 the diocese was combined with Gloucester and it was commonly said that Bristol had only half a cathedral and half a diocese!

This early photograph shows the late Norman Abbey gateway with the Dean's house on the left and the Precentor's house on the right. Part of the Deanery was demolished in the 1860s when Deanery Road was created and the rest went shortly after 1901 to make way for the new Central Library; the Precentor's house was carefully removed when the gateway was restored in 1885. (J.W.G. Gutch)

Bristol Cathedral, c. 1910. The cathedral was restored and considerably enlarged from the late 1860s. Much restoration of the old fabric was carried out, but it was the addition of a nave and two western towers designed by G.E. Street which transformed the exterior, giving Bristol, at last, a cathedral befitting the city. Work began in 1868 and the nave was completed in 1877, and the towers in 1888, although without the steeples of Street's design.

St Mary Magdelene (Church of England), Stoke Bishop, *c.* 1875. This church, designed by John Norton, was built in 1860 to provide a parish church for the growing population of Stoke Bishop. The tower and spire were added in 1872. Members of the Wills family and Sir George White, director of the tramway company and founder of the Bristol Aircraft Company, are buried in the churchyard.

Interior of Emmanuel church (Church of England), Guthrie Road, Clifton, *c.* 1910. Another design by John Norton, this Anglican church close to Clifton College was consecrated in 1869. A large tower was subsequently added but plans for a spire were never realised; the church no longer exists although the tower is incorporated in a modern block of flats called Emmanuel Court.

St Mary Redcliffe, *c*. 1875. The church lost its first spire in a storm in 1445 and the capstone of the replacement was laid by the mayor W. Proctor Baker in May 1872.

St John's (Church of England), Bedminster, before 1857. This old parish church, which the Bristol historian John Latimer described in 1887 as a 'mean edifice of the seventeenth century, capable of holding only 450 persons' was replaced by a new larger church, an example of High Victorian Gothic by John Norton. The last service in the old church was held on 25 June 1854 and it was demolished in 1857 after the replacement had been consecrated.

St Andrew's church, Clifton, c. 1910. This was the parish church of Clifton. It was designed by James Foster and built in 1819–22 replacing a seventeenth-century church, itself the replacement of an earlier church. The church was badly damaged in the Blitz on the night of 24 November 1940, and although the 112 ft high tower survived it was pulled down in 1954.

Interior of St Mary's-on-the-Quay (Roman Catholic), Colston Avenue, *c.* 1910. This church with its impressive Corinthian portico has been a familiar landmark on the Quay, and subsequently Colston Avenue, since 1839. It was designed by Richard Shackleton Pope as a chapel for the Irvingites – an evangelical sect – but shortly after its construction was purchased by the Roman Catholic Church. The interior, seen here, is no less impressive with giant columns dominating the chancel.

Greenbank Cemetery, *c.* 1912. This cemetery, belonging to St Philip's parish, was consecrated on 14 April 1871 and extended in 1880. The chapel with its polygonal turret was designed by Henry Masters and built in 1870. It came under municipal control in 1896 when the City Council became the burial board for the entire city.

Buckingham Baptist chapel, Queen's Road, *c.* 1910. Designed by Richard Shackleton Pope, this church, built in the continental High Gothic manner and opened on 2 June 1847, was described by one critic as 'a particularly chaste and beautiful Gothic building'.

Arley chapel (Congregational), Cheltenham Road, *c.* 1905. Here the architects, Foster & Wood, resorted to the Italianate for this Congregational church built in 1855 to serve new suburbs north of the centre. It now serves as a Polish church.

Western College, Cotham Road, *c.* 1910. Western College was founded to train Congregational ministers; this attractive example of Edwardian Jacobean architecture designed by H. Dare Bryan was opened on 27 September 1906. A similar training institution for the Baptists was established at Stokes Croft and moved to Woodland Road in 1915. The building now serves as a family practice.

Salvation Army Citadel, Ashley Road, built in 1896. The fortress-like Salvation Army headquarters was built in 1896, the centre of operations for General Booth's army – saving souls amongst the 'submerged tenth' of the population; those who somehow existed on incomes below the subsistence level. In 1881 the Salvation Army claimed 15.4 per cent of the church-going population in Bristol.

James Cox (1838–1900), home missionary,
c. 1890. Born at Westbury, Wiltshire, James
Cox worked as a furnace man at the Ashton
Ironworks until a foundry explosion left him
crippled and blind. He spent nearly a year
recovering from his injuries at the Bristol
General Hospital, an experience that changed
his life: previously a heavy drinker and keeper of
bad company he turned to Christianity. Upon
his recovery he was led on crutches to a
Wesleyan chapel in Bedminster; he learned to
read type for the blind and started work as a
missionary, visiting the sick and blind and
holding prayer meetings in his small terraced
house – 30 Sion Road, Bedminster. He also held
open-air meetings at which he played hymns on
a portable harmonium (now preserved at Blaise
Castle House Museum, Bristol), and with others
founded a mission band which as the Cycle
Mission Band was continued by one of his sons.
It is seen here in the early 1900s.

CORPORATE BRISTOL

The second half of the nineteenth century saw a greater involvement of local government in the running of the city. The Municipal Corporations Act of 1835 had transferred existing responsibilities for law and order from the old parish authorities to the City Council. From the mid-nineteenth century new national legislation invested the Council with new responsibilities: for health (for example, building sewers and public baths), enforcing building regulations, and maintaining parks, libraries, the Museum and the Art Gallery. The Council also assumed control of cemeteries in 1896 and after the Education Act of 1902 took over the running of schools. Each function was managed by its own committee, and after 1850 these multiplied so that by the early twentieth century there were thirty running the city's affairs.

Through the second half of the nineteenth century Bristol's leading industrialists such as Christopher Thomas, soap maker, and Thomas Proctor, bone merchant and dealer in manure, dominated local government, chairing committees and serving as aldermen and mayor. Until 1882 only those owning property worth more than £1,000 or occupying property of a rateable value of £30 or more were eligible for election. Before the Municipal Franchise Act of 1869 only about 3 to 10 per cent of the population were qualified to vote; thus a middle-class electorate produced a middle-class council. Boundary changes in the late nineteenth and early twentieth century increased the area governed by the city by over four times. The number of wards increased from ten in the 1850s to twenty three by 1907, whilst the number of elected councillors rose from forty-eight to sixty-nine although the distribution of councillors was uneven, favouring the prosperous and influential wards like Clifton. Nevertheless, as the vote was progressively extended, the Council became less socially exclusive and came to represent a wider cross-section of Bristol's population.

The City Council's officials were surrounded by a considerable degree of civic tradition and ceremony which had its roots in Bristol's medieval local government, although following the reforms of 1835 the number of ceremonial officials was reduced to make financial savings. The post of City Crier was abolished in 1890 and the office of Exchange Keeper in 1893. The Council did not invest in new council offices like so many other Victorian towns and cities, and had to squeeze its expanding business into the small and inconvenient Council House of 1825, which occupied a less than imposing site in Corn Street. However, the city acquired a new impressive Mansion House, the home of the mayor, in Clifton Down in 1874 thanks to the gift of Alderman Thomas Proctor, and in 1899 civic prestige was further strengthened when Queen Victoria conferred the title of Lord Mayor upon Sir Herbert Ashman, an honour already bestowed on the mayor of Birmingham and several other northern towns.

The Municipal Corporations Act of 1835 ordered boroughs throughout England and Wales to appoint a paid professional police force. The new force was established in 1836 with 227 officers led by a superintendent based at four police stations at Wine Street, Bedminster, Brandon Hill and Trinity Road, St Philips. A new central police station was built at the Bridewell in 1844, and the same year the river police was formed to protect merchant shipping and protect cargoes from fire and theft. In the late 1870s the police took over responsibility for fire protection throughout the city from the insurance companies, and a new city fire brigade was established with its own superintendent and twelve policemen. In 1880 the first full time detective staff – one inspector and seven detectives – were appointed. As the city grew, new police stations were added in the suburbs and allotted to the original four divisions. 'A' Division included the Bridewell station, the Water Police and Horfield station; 'B' Division comprised Bedminster, Brislington and Knowle; 'C' Division came to include Brandon Hill, Westbury-on-Trym, Redland, Stoke Bishop, Shirehampton and Avonmouth; whilst 'D' Division combined Trinity Road and stations at St George, Eastville and Fishponds. In 1898 the fire brigade was also expanded to cover the newly incorporated districts.

Hospital provision was already established in Bristol by the mid-nineteenth century but continued to expand to meet the demands of the growing population. The Society of Friends had established the General Hospital in a house in Guinea Street in 1832 with accommodation for thirty beds, but it was soon proving inadequate to treat the growing number of industrial accidents from the docks and from factories and collieries in Bedminster and Ashton. A new larger hospital was built from 1853 and when the main block opened in 1858 it had space for 150 beds, which was increased to 200 when a new wing was opened in 1891. The Bristol Royal Infirmary, founded in 1735, also increased its capacity in the later nineteenth century. By the early twentieth century the hospital was heavily in debt; it was rescued from its difficulties by Sir George White, managing director of the Bristol Tramways & Carriage Company, following his election as President and Treasurer in 1904. White organised an energetic programme of fund raising to clear the debt and also to finance the building of a new extension, a plain and uncompromisingly modern block designed by Charles Holden which was named the Edward VII Memorial Infirmary and opened on 28 June 1912. Support from leading industrial and commercial figures like White was an important factor in the expansion of hospital provision in Victorian and Edwardian Bristol. The Children's Hospital on St Michael's Hill largely owed its existence to the efforts of Mark Whitwill; and Joseph Storrs Fry, who served as President of the General Hospital, provided financial support together with E.P. Wills towards establishing the Queen Victoria Convalescent Home on Durdham Down, opened by the Queen in 1899.

In the mid-nineteenth century the care of the destitute, the old and infirm, the mentally ill and others unable to look after themselves rested with three Poor Law Unions – for Bristol, Bedminster and Clifton – and each had its own workhouse to provide indoor relief. The Bristol authority, the Board of Guardians, was established in 1696 and had adapted an ornate timber-framed merchant's house, St Peter's Hospital, as the city's workhouse and lunatic asylum. In the 1830s, to relieve severe overcrowding in St Peter's Hospital, a former prison for French prisoners of war at Stapleton was obtained for use as a workhouse. The Bedminster and Clifton Unions, which were also responsible for poor relief in some of the neighbouring rural parishes, established workhouses at Flax Bourton and Eastville. In 1898 a new Union for the whole of Bristol came into being, and that year there were 2,357 inmates in the workhouses formerly administered by the old authorities.

That same year, 1898, the twenty-two almshouses scattered across the city provided homes for 377 people. No other British city was so well provided with such charitable institutions: some had medieval origins – like Foster's almshouses, dating to 1483, whilst Lady Haberfield's almshouses in Hotwells were founded in 1891. The founders often aimed to benefit a particular type of person – thus Sarah Ridley's almshouses founded in 1739 were expressly for bachelors and spinsters. The Blue Maids' Orphanage had been founded in 1795 to care for some forty orphan girls: photographs of the orphanage in the 1890s are featured in this section, but at the time it was overshadowed by the considerably larger orphanage on Ashley Down founded by the Rev. George Muller in 1849, which housed 2,000 children by the 1880s.

In 1870, the year of the Education Act, a survey into educational provision in Bristol recorded 236 elementary schools in Bristol; the survey also highlighted the shortage of school places in the poorer parishes and estimated that about a third of children aged between five and ten years were not attending any school. By the terms of the 1870 Act a publicly elected school board with rate-aid was established in 1871, and immediately turned its attention to providing schools in the new industrial suburbs: in 1874 a school was built in St Philips, and the following year a school for 750 children was opened at Barton Hill. The new schools were undenominational – this was bitterly opposed by the Church of England and Conservatives – but some rudimentary teaching of the Bible was included in the curriculum and physical drill to promote proper conduct was instilled in a disciplined manner. Other Board schools were built in Bedminster, Ashton Gate, Hotwells, Redland and Baptist Mills, whilst some existing schools were taken over. By 1902, when the City Council took over responsibility for education from the School Board, average attendance was not far below 90 per cent.

There were several endowed schools providing secondary education, including the Queen Elizabeth's Hospital School and the Grammar School (see page 123). Both dated from the sixteenth century and acquired impressive buildings on new sites in the nineteenth century: Queen Elizabeth's Hospital was provided with a Tudor collegiate-style school on Brandon Hill, designed by Thomas Foster & Son and completed in 1847, whilst the Grammar School's new building at Tyndall's Park was opened in 1880. Clifton College was founded as a public school by the Clifton College Company. Charles Frederick Hansom designed the school, which opened in 1862 with fifty-eight boys; a handsome Gothic chapel was added four years later. Gothic architecture was considered appropriate for the education of young Christian gentlemen. The school's first headmaster, the Rev. John Percival, believed the school should serve the city at large and was closely involved in establishing the University, evening classes and missionary work amongst the poor.

The Lord Mayor's Chapel, College Green, *c.* 1912. Otherwise known as St Mark's, it was originally the chapel of the thirteenth-century Gaunt's Hospital. The chapel was purchased by the Corporation in 1541 and established as their official place of worship in 1722; it is the only civic church in the country. A thorough restoration in 1888–9 created its present-day external appearance.

The annual Rush Sunday Service at St Mary Redcliffe with the Lord Mayor, Edward Robinson, Whit-Sunday, 1909. The service is held in commemoration of William Canynge, a leading Bristol merchant of the fifteenth century who later entered the Church. A special service is preached in the presence of the Lord Mayor and rushes are strewn on the ground.

Ridleys Almshouse, Milk Street, *c.* 1900. Founded in 1739 by Sarah Ridley, this was one of over twenty almshouses in Bristol in the second half of the nineteenth century; in Mathew's 1864 Bristol Directory, it is described as having places for 'five bachelors and five maids', each receiving 9*s* fortnightly. The city watch box on the corner, used by nightwatchmen, was built in 1820 and demolished in August 1913 after a period of use as a shop.

Joseph Croot, City Crier from 1855 until 1890, when the post was abolished. He wore a livery of black coat with brass buttons bearing the Bristol coat of arms, tricorn hat, blue velvet breeches and gaiters.

Police Constabulary 'A'Division tug of war team, champions of the West of England and South Wales, 1907. 'A' Division was based at the Central Station, Bridewell. Back row from left, Ashford, PC Hook (Vice Capt.), PC Robbins, PC Froud; middle row: PS Hill (Trainer), PC Harding (Vice Capt.), PC Dyer, PC Gully, PC Grant, PS Clapp; seated: Inspector G. London, Mr C. Croker, Deputy Chief Constable, Mr J. Cann, Chief Constable, Inspector R. Pope, Inspector G. Harris (Capt.) The Chief Constable is wearing his day uniform. (R. Pratchett, 130 Cheltenham Road, Bristol)

Bristol Constabulary Fire Brigade, Central Station, 1882. Officers stand alongside their Merryweather horse-drawn steam fire engine: Engineer Prouting, left, Superintendent Wingfield, centre front, First Coachman Pearce holding the reins and Second Coachman Shipp on the right, and five officers: Wergen, Smith, James, Durrant and Martin (from left to right on the engine). Merryweather, an old-established London firm, were leading makers of fire engines. The type shown here used steam from the engine to drive the pump.

Bristol General Hospital, Guinea Street, *c.* 1910. This imposing building of grey Pennant stone and Bath stone was built from 1853 on the site of the former Guinea Street hospital established in 1830. Designed by W.B. Gingell, it was an early example of the 'Bristol Byzantine' style adopted for many large buildings in the city during the 1860s and 1870s. The basement formed dockside warehouses, which provided an extra source of income.

Prince – canine friend of the Bristol General Hospital. This dog, owned by Alfred William Collins, persuaded many customers entering his master's shellfish bar in Colston Avenue to make a donation in his collections box for the Royal General Hospital, and between 1915 and his death in 1924 raised over £37.

The Royal Hospital for Sick Children and Women, St Michael's Hill, 1890s. The hospital was established in 1866 to treat children under twelve years of age, women 'suffering from diseases peculiar to their sex' and to improve knowledge of child-care especially among the poor. Originally housed in the Royal Fort, the Gothic style premises shown here, designed by Robert Carwen, were built in 1885. In this photograph, convalescing children are seen on the lawn outside the hospital holding toys and dolls, with several nurses in attendance.

King Edward Memorial Building, Royal Infirmary, Upper Maudlin Street, c. 1915. This was one of the earliest of provincial hospitals, founded in 1735. Sir George White, the dynamic and forward thinking director of the tramway company, rescued the hospital from debt after he became President and Treasurer in 1904. With his backing this new large block, designed by H. Percy Adams and Charles Holden, was opened in 1912.

St Peter's Hospital, late nineteenth century. This remarkably ornate timber-framed house beside St Peter's church was first mentioned in 1402 and rebuilt in 1612 by Robert Aldworth, a prominent merchant and several times mayor. After serving as a mint during the re-coinage of 1696–8 it was then purchased by the Bristol Corporation of the Poor (i.e. the Board of Guardians responsible for poor relief) for use as a workhouse for the destitute and as a lunatic asylum. From the 1830s it was replaced by a larger workhouse at Stapleton and after 1865 used mainly for administrative purposes. It was destroyed during the Blitz of 24 November 1940 – arguably Bristol's greatest architectural loss of the Second World War.

Blue Coat School, Henbury, 1870s. A charity school founded in the early seventeenth century, which was rebuilt in 1830. In 1869 the school was providing elementary education for sixty boys including seven boarders. The 1871 national census records the master as Henry Pillenger, while there were seven 'boy scholars' aged between ten and fourteen boarding at the adjacent Henbury School House.

South Street Schools, Bedminster, c. 1912. Designed by the Bristol architect W. V. Gouch, this school was built by the Bristol School Board in 1894. It originally had nineteen classrooms and three separate yards for boys, girls and infants.

Blue Maids' Asylum for Poor Orphan Girls, Ashley Hill, 1890s. This orphanage was established in 1795 to 'rescue destitute girls from idleness and vice, qualifying them for servants in respectable families'. The building shown here was built in about 1828 and suggests that orphan girls here grew up in a much pleasanter environment than those living in George Muller's barracks-like orphanage on Ashley Down.

Morning lessons at Blue Maids' Orphanage, 1890s. The schoolmistress (see also opposite) is sitting on the left, some of the girls are sewing but others, holding slates, may be grappling with the arithmetic of the problem chalked on the blackboard. The 1891 national census records forty-two girls in the orphanage ranging in age from five to sixteen years. Embroidery made by the girls was sold to supplement the income from donations and legacies.

The kitchen, Blue Maids' Orphanage,1890s. It is 11.25 a.m., the cook is peeling apples and has the help of three girls who are probably glad to be spared the sewing and the arithmetic lesson. Compare the simple flat flame gas burner fitted here with the more ornate lamp in the study, which appears to be a combined paraffin and gas lamp.

The study or drawing room at Blue Maids' Orphanage, 1890s. The woman on the left is almost certainly Isolene Lee, a native of Weymouth born in about 1848, matron of the orphanage from 1887 to 1919; the woman netting on the right may be Anne Miller, who was the schoolmistress at the orphanage in 1891. The orphanage closed in about 1926.

Net practice at Clifton College, late 1860s. Sport became an important part of life in the school, and cricket the pre-eminent sport up to the First World War. The imposing Gothic buildings were designed by Charles Frederick Hansom, the Big School prominent in this view was opened in 1862 and the chapel completed in 1866; a tower and north aisle were added later to the chapel.

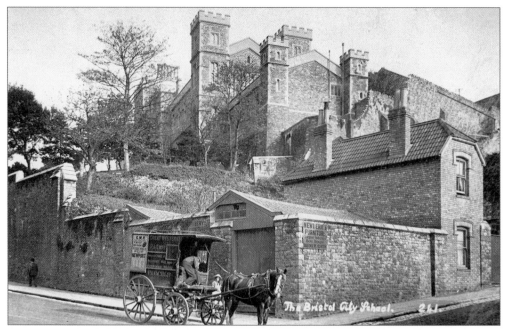

Queen Elizabeth Hospital School from the corner of Jacob's Wells Road and John Carr's Terrace, *c.* 1910. The City School or Queen Elizabeth's Hospital was founded by John Carr, an Elizabethan soap maker, in 1586. Built in 1847 of red Brandon grit from the site on which it was built, the school rises fortress-like on the western side of Brandon Hill. The red brick house, below, built in about 1894, provided accommodation for the school's stable keeper.

ARTS & LEISURE

T he modernisation of the city widened opportunities for leisure: new forms of entertainment and recreation were added to the old. Music halls, cinemas, parks and open spaces were created and new cultural facilities such as libraries, a museum and an art gallery established. There were several major factors governing the rise of new types of leisure: technological innovations, higher levels of popular education and, as in other areas of the city's development, leisure also benefited from greater municipal involvement.

There were inevitably social differences in forms of leisure and entertainment. The appeal of the theatre was strongest amongst the middle classes: thus the New Theatre Royal opened in Park Row by James Henry Shute, owner of the Theatre Royal, who recognised the demand from theatre-goers in the fashionable suburbs for a theatre closer to home than the old Theatre Royal in King Street. Better known as the Princes Theatre, it became Bristol's most fashionable theatre. In the mid-nineteenth century the recreation and entertainment of poorer citizens centred on drink, informal activities and occasional visits from fairs and circuses. The new forms of leisure, however, saw greater formality as halls were established for the performance of more organised entertainments. The largest and most important was Colston Hall, opened in 1867, which became the focal point of musical life in the city. The increasing mass appeal of music was also reflected by the rise of the music hall. The earliest were tavern music halls: they served drink and were the subject of disapproval from Nonconformists and the Temperance movement, but in the 1890s the reputation of music halls was transformed by the opening of the People's Palace, Baldwin Street, and the Empire Theatre in Old Market. Unlike the tavern music halls they were teetotal – although entrance to the Empire Theatre, Old Market, was through the doors of a public house – the White Hart! The old music halls could not compete: the last to go was the Tivoli in

Broadmead, which ran into financial difficulties and closed in 1900. The new music halls were respectable; they were family places of entertainment and with seating capacities of about 3,000 they had to have a broad appeal. With them the age of popular mass entertainment had arrived.

The music halls were also the first establishments to introduce a new novelty – the cinematograph. The last of the old tavern music halls, the Tivoli, was the first to show the moving picture in 1896. They were soon being shown at other venues including the Colston Hall and the People's Palace, and from 1908 purpose-built cinemas appeared, the first being the Bio in Counterslip; thereafter the popularity of the cinema increased rapidly and by 1919 there were some thirty-four across the city.

Greater organisation also permeated sport. Team games like cricket, rugby football and association football increased in popularity within a framework of regional and nationally recognised leagues. The growth of organised sports was helped by shorter working hours, improvements in transport and also by cheap press and sporting publications which generated popular interest. Cycling was another pastime which benefited from improvements in the design of the bicycle. Archery and tennis also became popular from the 1870s – with women as well as men, although sports that required equipment tended to remain the preserve of the middle classes. Association football, however, enjoyed widespread appeal, and from the 1880s developed as the spectator sport of the urban masses.

The involvement of municipal government in providing parks and public baths was born of the concern for the health of citizens living in areas of dense housing. Parks were established by the City Council, particularly from the 1880s, until by the early 1900s there were thirty-eight parks, open spaces and commons maintained by the city. New parks such as the 70 acres of Eastville Park, acquired in 1887, and Victoria Park in Bedminster (see page 57), 57 acres in extent, provided important green spaces within a smoke-filled, crowded industrial environment. Besides providing fresh air, parks were used for physical exercise whilst music could be enjoyed from a bandstand – a common feature of the Victorian park. Swimming baths were originally seen as a way of keeping the working classes clean, and then interest in swimming as a sport emerged in the 1870s; the Council built prestigious new baths at Jacobs Wells in 1884. Municipal administration was next extended to the arts when the Council assumed control of the Museum in 1894, and in 1905 the Art Gallery, the gift of Lord Winterstoke to the city, was opened.

Royal West of England Academy, Queen's Road, 1870s. This Italianate building designed by John Hirst was built in 1854 for the joint use of the Bristol Academy of Fine Arts and the Bristol Society of Architects.

Ernest Board (1877–1934) painting the marriage of William Penn and Hannah Callowhill at the Friends' Meeting House, the Friary, Bristol, completed in 1916. Board lived at The Elms, Ashley Hill. He was a prolific artist in oils and watercolours, and his paintings of great moments in the history of Bristol reflected Bristol's civic pride in the early twentieth century.

View from the stage in the Princes Theatre, Park Row, *c.* 1910. Opened as the New Theatre Royal in 1867 by James Henry Shute, owner of the Theatre Royal, as a response to the demand from theatre-goers in the fashionable suburbs for a theatre closer to home than the old Theatre Royal in King Street. It became Bristol's most fashionable theatre, but was destroyed by enemy action in 1940.

Colston Hall, *c.* 1910. The Colston Hall Co. was launched in the mid-1860s to provide Bristol with a large concert hall capable of taking the large orchestras then on tour. The building designed by Foster & Wood was finally opened on 20 September 1867 and W.H. Wills provided the organ, which cost £3,000. The hall gave a great boost to the musical life of the city, and in 1873 Bristol held its first music festival.

The Coliseum Picture House, Park Row, one of Bristol's early cinemas. It opened in August 1912 but did not survive the arrival of the 'talkies' in the 1920s. It was also used as a skating rink and dance hall, and during the First World War seaplanes for the Admiralty and Avro biplanes were assembled here by Parnall & Sons.

Bedminster Hippodrome, East Street, c. 1911. This imposing music hall seating 3,000 was opened by Walter de Freece in July 1911, but soon ran into difficulties and was taken over by Oswald Stoll, builder of the new Bristol Hippodrome, St Augustine's Parade; he converted it to a cinema in May 1915 and in March 1918 it was renamed the Stoll Picture House – one of five cinemas in the Bedminster area by 1919. The constable is from 'B' Division based in Bedminster.

Street organ in St Philip's Marsh, *c*. 1905. Music was an important feature of popular street entertainment until finally drowned out by the noise of motor vehicle traffic during the 1920s.

Entrance lodge to the Zoological gardens, Clifton, *c*. 1915. The gardens, occupying 12 acres, were established by the Bristol & Clifton Zoological Society in 1835. The original subscribers included I.K. Brunel, W.D. & H.O. Wills, members of the Fry family and John Harford of Blaise Castle House, Henbury (see page 84).

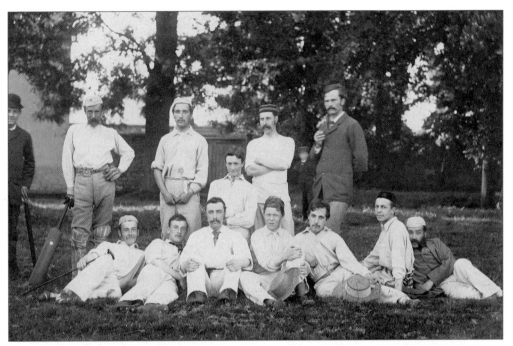

Gentlemen cricketers of the Rockleaze cricket team, *c.* 1875. Cricket flourished in Victorian Bristol, particularly in the affluent suburbs.

St Philip's Football Club, 1906. The popularity of association football was strongest in the industrial suburbs. Henry Webb, son of the landlord of the Victoria, St Philip's Marsh, and later landlord himself of the Rising Sun, Lower Castle Street, is on the middle row, second left.

John Webb, landlord of the Victoria, with his wife Mary in a donkey and trap outside the back door of the public house in Victoria Terrace, St Philip's Marsh, *c.* 1909.

An Edwardian picnic: Dorothy (left) and Frances Brewer (second from right) with their mother of 6 West Park, Cotham, and two friends, Connie Stroud and Kathleen Bishop, *c.* 1910.

BRISTOL & THE GREAT WAR

War with Germany was declared on 4 August 1914. It was holiday time. Excursion trains were cancelled to enable the movement of troops; soldiers of the Gloucestershire Regiment based at Horfield Barracks, the Territorial Forces and members of the Royal Naval Reserve were mobilised immediately. The one German ship in the port was seized and her crew detained. Amongst the civilian population, the fear that food would soon run out caused panic: there were queues at the shops and prices rose. The fears, however, were unfounded as the Government moved quickly to control prices.

Over the next four years, until the signing of the Armistice on 11 November 1918, Bristol played a major part in what quickly became the 'Great War'. Unprecedented in its world-wide repercussions and in many ways novel, it was the first to be fought by the entire nation and not merely the armed forces. For the first time, the highly organised states of the twentieth century were able to command the energies of all citizens to mobilise the productive capacity of modern industries towards the war effort and also to call upon the resources of modern technology to find new methods of destruction and defence. Many Bristolians were directly involved in the military effort: some 60,000 men from Bristol served in the wars and at least 4,000 were killed. Rolls of honour became a regular feature of church services whilst the *Western Daily Press* carried hundreds of obituaries of men killed in the fighting. Many women were enrolled into national service and served in the hospitals caring for the wounded; within the first month of the war, trained nurses from the Royal Infirmary were dispatched for service at the front.

The first hospital train bringing wounded soldiers to the city arrived at Temple Meads on 2 September 1914, returning 120 men from Mons. They were treated at the Second Southern Hospital set up by the War Office, which consisted of the new wing of the Royal Infirmary opened in 1912 together with a new infirmary at Southmead; it was soon augmented by Bishop's Knoll in Stoke Bishop, the home of Robert and Margery Bush which they converted to a hospital of a hundred beds. In 1916 the Red Maids' School at Westbury-on-Trym was converted to a hospital and auxiliary hospitals under the Red Cross were set up in the Bristol area. Many voluntary organisations, besides, assisted in the care of the sick and wounded.

The war saw a huge increase in incoming tonnage through the port from foreign countries: the wounded returned on hospital ships through the port whilst troops and equipment were dispatched by sea – the port played a significant role, for example, in supplying the Gallipoli expedition in 1915. Many local industries contributed to the war effort. Shipbuilding in Bristol was not in a thriving state in 1914 but by 1916 the need to replace shipping lost to German submarine attacks generated new work. Charles Hill & Sons, the city's leading shipbuilders, constructed additional berths at their Albion yard to cope with the extra demand. The city's newly established aero industry also played a major role. The British and Colonial Aeroplane Company, established only four years before war broke out, manufactured hundreds of aircraft for use during the war including 376 Bristol Scouts and the versatile Bristol Fighter, which played an important part in the later stages of the war. From 1915 the Bristol firm Parnall & Sons commenced aircraft manufacture, using the Coliseum in Park Row for assembly. Douglas Motors Ltd supplied motocycles for war use. John Lysaght Ltd, manufacturers of galvanised iron, made thousands of Nissen huts, wire netting and other galvanised ware. Christopher Thomas & Bros and other soap makers produced dynamite glycerine and the Bristol Gas Company supplied benzol and toluol for use in high explosives. Wills and Fry's turned to the manufacture of shells whilst their tobacco and chocolate was sent to the troops on the front. The clothing manufacturers and boot makers in the district supplied military clothing; it was reckoned that some three to four million Bristol-made boots were supplied to troops worldwide. Women took the place of men who had gone to war: they were introduced on the trams in December 1916 and by March 1917 the Bristol Tramways & Carriage Company had 800 women filling men's places.

When news of an armistice reached the city, there was spontaneous public rejoicing. Many people imagined that life would settle down to something like it had been before, but with the Great War a whole epoch had come to an end.

Soldiers marching in Park Row as passengers on board a tram from Westbury-on-Trym look on, 7 September 1914. According to the reverse inscription of this postcard, these were students from the University 'marching to camp at Barrow'. The Coliseum in the background was soon to be used for the assembly of fighter aircraft.

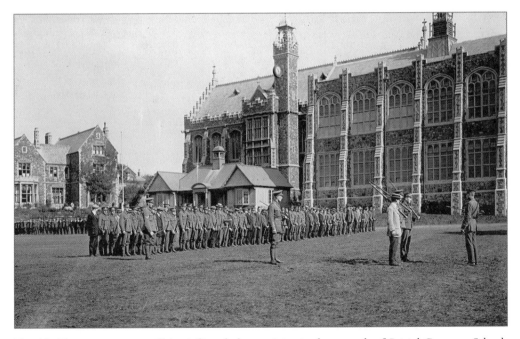

The 4th Gloucesters, some still in civilian clothes, training in the grounds of Bristol Grammar School, 1914. The school voluntarily gave up its playing field in Tyndall's Park, which was used extensively for training purposes.

Margery and Robert Bush who converted their home, Bishop's Knoll in Stoke Bishop, to a wartime hospital at their own expense. It received its first patients from 13 September 1914 and was the only privately owned hospital in the country to receive wounded soldiers directly from the Front.

The Motor Cycle Club taking convalescing soldiers for a ride, c. 1919. The King Edward Memorial Building became part of the War Office's Second Southern Hospital on the outbreak of the First World War and treated 20,000 sick and wounded soldiers as in-patients and 50,000 as out-patients. Organised outings to the country, the zoo, the Museum and Art Gallery and local music halls were arranged to give recovering soldiers a change of scenery.

Captured German submarines U86 and UC92 on view to the public in St Augustine's Reach in December 1918. German submarines caused extensive loss of allied shipping during the war, including merchant vessels and hospital ships on their way to Bristol.

Bristol Peace Celebrations Certificate presented to all schoolchildren in Bristol on 24 July 1919.

ACKNOWLEDGEMENTS

Most of the photographs are from the collections of Bristol Museums & Art Gallery. The photographs on page 105 are reproduced by kind permission of Avon & Somerset Constabulary. I am grateful to my colleagues at Bristol Museums & Art Gallery for their support, and particularly to Paul Elkin and Andy King; special thanks are due to Francis Greenacre who made many useful suggestions to the text. I am also grateful to the staff of the Bristol Record Office for permission to reproduce the photographs on page 4, 14 top, 23, 68 top, 69 top, 75, 80 bottom, 91 top, 94 top, and especially to Alison Brown who helped identify Thomas Denford and George King in the photographs.

Primary sources used included parliamentary reports into sanitary conditions in 1845 and manufactures in 1866, local newspapers, trade directories, census returns, building plan records; port records and the Fry's business archive in the BRO. There is a huge literature on Bristol and many published books and articles were consulted: below is a brief list of those which proved to be invaluable in preparing this book.

Anderson, C., *A City and its Cinemas*, Redcliffe, 1983

Bettey, J.H., *Bristol Observed*, Redcliffe, 1986

Bishop, I.S., *The City & Kingswood Line, A History of Bristol's Trams*, Bishop, 1995

Cohen, L., *Greater Bristol by Lesser Columbus*, Pelham Press, 1893

Crick, C., *Victorian Buildings in Bristol*, Redcliffe, 1975

Dresser, M. & Ollenshaw, P., *The Making of Modern Bristol*, Redcliffe, 1996

Elkin, P., *Images of Maritime Bristol*, Breedon, 1995

Harvey, C. & Press, J., *Studies in the Business History of Bristol*, Bristol Academic Press, 1988

Jones, D., *A History of Clifton*, Phillimore, 1992

Latimer, J., *Annals of Bristol, Nineteenth Century, 1887*, reprinted Kingsmead, 1970

Little, B., *The Story of Bristol*, Redcliffe, 1991

Mallory, K., *The Bristol House*, Redcliffe, 1985

Mellor, H.E., *Leisure and the Changing City*, Routledge & Kegan Paul, 1976

Stone, G.F., *Bristol As It Was – And As It Is*, Walter Reid, 1909

Wells, C., & Stone, G.F., *Bristol and the Great War*, Arrowsmith, 1920

White, G., *Tramlines to the Stars*, Redcliffe, 1995

Many of the pamphlets published by the Bristol Branch of the Historical Association were also valuable sources of information and the many photograph compilations by Reece Winstone were also useful.